# So, I'm Autistic

*of related interest*

**The Young Autistic Adult's Independence Handbook**
*Haley Moss*
ISBN 978 1 78775 757 8
eISBN 978 1 78775 758 5

**Looking After Your Autistic Self**
A Personalised Self-Care Approach to Managing
Your Sensory and Emotional Well-Being
*Niamh Garvey*
ISBN 978 1 83997 560 8
eISBN 978 1 83997 561 5

**Nurturing Your Autistic Young Person**
A Parent's Handbook to Supporting Newly Diagnosed Teens and Pre-Teens
*Cathy Wassell*
*Foreword by Emily Burke*
*Illustrated by Eliza Fricker*
ISBN 978 1 83997 111 2
eISBN 978 1 83997 112 9

**The Guide to Good Mental Health on the Autism Spectrum**
*Yenn Purkis, Emma Goodall and Jane Nugent*
*Forewords by Wenn Lawson and Kirsty Dempster-Rivett*
ISBN 978 1 84905 670 0
eISBN 978 1 78450 195 2

# So, I'm Autistic

An Introduction to Autism for
Young Adults and Late Teens

## Sarah O'Brien

**Jessica Kingsley Publishers**
London and Philadelphia

First published in Great Britain in 2023 by Jessica Kingsley Publishers
An imprint of John Murray Press

2

Copyright © Sarah O'Brien 2023

The right of Sarah O'Brien to be identified as the Author
of the Work has been asserted by her in accordance with
the Copyright, Designs and Patents Act 1988.

A CIP catalogue record for this title is available from
the British Library and the Library of Congress

ISBN 978 1 83997 226 3
eISBN 978 1 83997 227 0

Printed and bound in Great Britain by Clays Ltd

Jessica Kingsley Publishers' policy is to use papers that are natural,
renewable and recyclable products and made from wood grown
in sustainable forests. The cover is printed on uncoated board to
eliminate the use of plastic in the manufacturing of this book. The
logging and manufacturing processes are expected to conform
to the environmental regulations of the country of origin.

Jessica Kingsley Publishers
Carmelite House
50 Victoria Embankment
London EC4Y 0DZ

www.jkp.com

John Murray Press
Part of Hodder & Stoughton Limited
An Hachette UK Company

—

*For Jamie, who continues to accompany
me through a lifetime of thoughts*

# Acknowledgements

Writing isn't a solitary task; it's the conversations that per-colate as thoughts that become words on a page. I'd like to thank Hannah for helping to drag me through university so I could write about it, Emily for showing me what inclusive workplaces can be like, and Juli for showing me what friends are for.

I want to thank the group chat (Amy, Rachel, Ginny, Caroline, and Marie) for providing a space where I can explore ideas around writing, disability, and society.

For Sara and Holly, who pushed me to write with autistic authenticity, thank you for reminding me that I'm writing for all of us. Thank you for reminding me that we can and should take up space rather than make ourselves smaller or more palatable to audiences who won't love us anyway.

For my family, who didn't always understand what I was writing at times, thank you for listening and encouraging me at every step even when it felt insurmountable at times.

For Jamie, who is constantly building up the ground beneath me and never letting me turn back, thank you for believing in me even when I don't.

For Glenn, Oli, and Colin, thank you for letting me take the space I need to write alongside juggling my studies.

# Contents

## Part III: Finding Out More

# Introduction

As I write this book, I'm a 26-year-old autistic adult, I've known I'm autistic for nearly a decade, and I've lived for eight years with this diagnosis. Unfortunately, I've struggled through many years to get to the point of knowing how to exist in a world not built for us. Negotiating the frankly colossal mountain of change in your late teens on the way to becoming an adult is difficult enough; add on an autism diagnosis and life gets even harder.

Sadly, there isn't a secret manual outlining exactly how to get through it, though it feels like everyone else has one. We can only take leaps of faith – lots of them and not always with a lot of confidence or faith in those leaps. We all must face far too many of these leaps, unless, of course, we have people to support and guide us, telling us what we need to know. Unfortunately, that can be the tricky part to navigate: what do we need to know? That's what this book aims to do: provide a script or support for how to do what adulthood will make you do anyway, in a way that is more accessible for you.

You might be reading this book to find out more about autism after a diagnosis yourself, or maybe you're the parent of someone recently diagnosed. This book is written entirely from an autistic perspective, by someone still clinging onto and trying to navigate their way through young adulthood. Spoiler: it's me.

Throughout this book, I draw upon my own autistic experiences, both personal and professional. They include struggling with the social pressures of school and the crushing weight of mental health issues that I couldn't alleviate alone. Then, receiving an autism diagnosis aged 18 and navigating the move into adulthood through university, employment, relationships, and everything else I came across on my journey. As well as reflections and advice based on my personal experience of autism, this book contains the knowledge that I've gained from from working with autistic children and young people since 2015 and working in autism and disability research since 2016.

I've intentionally spent my time personally and professionally building my knowledge of autism from the perspectives of autistic people of all ages and backgrounds. My expertise isn't a fluke; it's hard-earned, and it informs every word of this book. In the following chapters, I weave together my personal experiences, my experience of helping others, and the knowledge I have gained through working in and around autism for seven years. So, trust me, you're in safe hands.

To start our journey together, I should probably share my thoughts on things relevant to autistic culture. These ideas are contentious and have been debated throughout history within the autistic and autism communities.[1] This doesn't mean that my views and perspectives are right, proper, or correct. Instead, I like to think these views have been suitably shaped over time by every autistic person I've encountered, and their viewpoints are evident in the book.

## Identity-first or person-first?

Identity-first language means someone's identity (disability, sexuality, race, ethnicity, or religion) is said or written before the word 'person'. Sometimes, the identity is said without being followed by the word 'person'. Examples of this include 'Deaf person', 'bisexual', 'Black person', 'Irish person', or 'Catholic'.

---

1   The autistic community includes autistic people. The autism community is a bit wider and includes family members of autistic people, professionals that work with autistic people, and those whose careers include autism as a focus (e.g., charities, researchers).

Person-first language relates to when the word 'person' is said or written in a sentence before the person's identity. Examples of this include things like 'a person with cancer' or 'a person with brown hair'. Typically for learning disabilities, there is a preference for person-first language ('person with a learning disability or learning difficulty').

In the UK, according to disability scholars and disability activists, disabled people generally prefer to be called a disabled person rather than a person with a disability. The United Nations and the Paralympics use person-first language, which means they use 'people with disabilities' instead of 'disabled people'.[2]

Throughout this book, I will use identity-first language ('autistic person') rather than person-first language ('person with autism' or 'person on the spectrum') to refer to autism. This is a personal preference of mine and is also a general preference as expressed by the autistic community. Lydia X. Z. Brown,[3] an autistic disability advocate based in America, has written about this subject for the Autistic Self Advocacy Network much more eloquently than I ever could. On their blog, they have written extensively and in an accessible way about this topic and more. Their work is well worth a deep dive. Research has also been conducted on this topic in 2016 with autistic people, parents, and professionals by Lorcan Kenny with colleagues from the charity, healthcare, and academic sectors.[4] The results of their research indicated a general preference for 'autistic person' amongst autistic people and their family members, but many professionals continue to use

2   If you're interested in finding out more, the National Center on Disability and Journalism, based at Arizona State University, have a Disability Language Style Guide that talks through some of the ways different disabilities and conditions can or should be spoken about.
3   You can find up-to-date information from Lydia on their Twitter account @autistichoya.
4   Kenny, L., Hattersley, C., Molins, B., Buckley, C., Povey, C., & Pellicano, E. (2016). Which terms should be used to describe autism? Perspectives from the UK autism community. *Autism, 20*(4), 442–462. https://doi.org/10.1177/1362361315588200

'person with autism'. I appreciate that this takes a view from the English language that might not mesh with the grammar and language rules of different languages and cultures.

For me, there is nothing wrong or bad about being autistic, nor can it be separated from any thought I have or action that I take. Ultimately, for me, autism frames my entire way of being, whether I consciously think about it or not. Therefore, I am an autistic person, not a person with autism. I can take my glasses off, but I can't take my autism off. I can dye my hair another colour, but I can't change that I'm autistic. Recognizing that autism isn't a bad thing changed everything for me. My diagnosis started off negatively with the clinicians' words, but learning about autism from autistic people who didn't see themselves as inadequate or broken saved me. Sometimes the goodness of you gets drowned out by the world screaming that something about you is wrong. So now, I wear my identity with pride. I am autistic, and those who made me feel bad about myself can't win by shaping my identity for me. I think of my identity as a political statement, but that isn't how everyone feels about their identity.

Each person has the right to define themselves however they choose; that choice is theirs, not the choice of others. Some prefer person-first language, others prefer identity-first, and some don't mind either. While my preference is to use 'autistic' to describe myself (which is partially why this book is called *So, I'm Autistic*), how you express yourself is ultimately your choice. Please don't let anyone ever take away your choice. Your choice of identity and defining yourself is not stagnant and can change as you grow and shift in your identity. You have the right to be represented using the terms you choose. You're allowed to be selfish about this, trust me.

While everyone can choose the terms with which to define themselves, there is also no denying the power and importance of words. Words shape how we think, how others think, and the way that we develop ideas about topics. If you always hear a word in a negative context, you start to think about that word, idea, or concept negatively. In my personal experience, person-first language has generally been used to hurt me, and identity-first language has been used to affirm or lift me up. This isn't a perfect distinction because I know 'autistic' has been used as an insult, but it is a binary that sort of works.

Similarly, 'gay' was also thrown around as an insult while I was at school. There was – and maybe still is – a time when 'Don't be so autistic' was used to insult people and their actions. For me, it is a clear choice to affirm that autism is part of my identity, to challenge people if I hear them use it as an insult, and to strive to move to a point where there is less stigma around autism.

One defence of person-first language is that 'it puts the person first'. This is technically correct: that is the definition of person-first language. I then question why someone needs to be reminded of my personhood over and above anything else that might form part of my identity. To me, it feels like someone is attempting to separate what they, a non-autistic person, see as a negative identity from my humanity. Through the very act of trying to focus on me as a person, they manage to dehumanize me by trying to separate me from something that sits at the core of everything I am. The act of calling me a 'person with autism' instantly signals to me that the person views autism as something that should be distanced from me as a person and that they attach some stigma to autistic expression.

### Autism spectrum condition or autism spectrum disorder: how to refer to autism

I prefer to use the term autism spectrum condition (ASC) rather than autism spectrum disorder (ASD). I also simply refer to autism as autism. There isn't technically a need for 'spectrum' or other descriptors.

Language like 'condition' is far less medical than 'disorder', which often has negative and disease-like connotations associated with it. Autism is not a medical illness, disease, or disorder, but a different way someone experiences and interacts with the world. Using the less medical framing of 'condition' when talking about autism rather than using 'disorder' can be a subtle positive shift. Disorder insinuates that something is wrong with someone. There is nothing wrong with or bad about being an autistic person. *There is nothing wrong with being autistic.*

Historically, the acronym for autism has been ASD. However, language is slowly shifting towards ASC, so you might see both used when autism is described in different scenarios and settings. Language is and always will be constantly changing and evolving. With increasing input from autistic people, we are moving from language that stigmatized us and was shaped by others to language that we are shaping and deciding upon ourselves.

## Functioning labels or just support needs

Alongside the shift from autism spectrum disorder to autism spectrum condition or just autism, there is also a shift in the language on the periphery of how autism and autistic people are spoken about. In previous times (although in some places this continues), autism was split neatly into 'high-functioning autism' and 'low-functioning autism'. This segregation or categorization has been used to show those who 'function well in society' and those who 'do not function in society'. This is an incredibly hazardous categorization and segregation of autistic people. Not just because our 'functioning' or capability shifts from day to day (sometimes even hour to hour or minute to minute), but also because it creates a hierarchy of autism that places some people higher than others.[5]

Instead of functioning labels, I use the term 'support needs' to talk about autistic people's needs, reasonable adjustments,

---

5    If you want to read more about this, I suggest searching for information about the hierarchy of impairment/disability, which highlights how damaging it can be.

and access needs. This term recognizes the fluctuations in these needs and that they are situational. This places emphasis on the fact that the environment needs to change to support the autistic person rather than the autistic person needing to change to fit the environment or society. It removes the responsibility from the autistic person and makes the responsibility for inclusion collective. A person may have high support needs when going to a new place but might have lower support needs doing something they are familiar with in a quiet environment. The words 'high' and 'low' remain; however, the stigma is removed, and the pressure offloaded from the autistic person and onto society instead.

Other previously used negative names for autism that split autism into levels are 'mild autism', 'moderate autism', and 'severe autism'. The thing is, we're not a spice chart, and there is no such thing as mild or severe. You're either autistic, or you're not. Someone can't be a little bit autistic or very autistic. It's a bit like pregnancy, in a way. Someone who is pregnant is pregnant no matter how far their pregnancy has progressed; they're never 'a little bit pregnant' they're simply pregnant or not. We might know or experience traits related to pregnancy but aren't pregnant unless we are growing a child. Both pregnant and non-pregnant people might experience nausea in the mornings, and both autistic people and non-autistic people may have sensory sensitivities or difficulty socializing.

You might hear many ways – a spectrum of ways you could say – of talking about autism, and at the root of it all, a lot of these are euphemisms for autism. They are usually people trying to talk around the subject or trying to talk about autism in a way they think is positive or trying to distance *your autism* from the negative image of autism they have in their head.

## Is autism gendered?

Throughout the history of autism, there have generally been more boys or men diagnosed as autistic than there have been girls or women. In previous research and estimates, this ratio has been about 16 autistic men for every 1 autistic woman. This ratio changed depending on which co-occurring conditions were included. Often this ratio was found to be nearer to equal when considering autistic people with a learning disability. More recently, the ratio of autistic men to autistic women has become more gender balanced. Research from 2017 estimates the ratio is closer to three autistic men for every autistic woman.[6]

While these ratios show us that more women have received an autism diagnosis in recent years compared to when autism was previously viewed as a male-dominated diagnosis, it often brings up questions about why. Why have more men been diagnosed than women? Why are women suddenly being diagnosed? Why aren't those who don't fit this constructed gender binary included in these statistics?

Without delving too much into it, the definitions of autism came from research focused primarily on boys, which then formed the diagnostic criteria. Professionals continued to use this framework and way of thinking about autism for many decades. Eventually, understanding began to shift in the 2000s and 2010s; suddenly, women and girls began to be proactively recognized and diagnosed. Those who were 'obviously' autistic, who neatly fit into the diagnostic criteria, were probably being diagnosed all along. Now those who hid in plain sight or presented a different version of autism were being diagnosed. What this really means is, some people have traditionally had an easier time accessing diagnosis, and others have had and continue to have much more challenging experiences. Unfortunately, the challenge of accessing an autism diagnosis is not just a gendered issue, it also has different impacts depending

---

6    Loomes, R., Hull, L., & Mandy, W. P. L. (2017). What is the male-to-female ratio in autism spectrum disorder? A systematic review and meta-analysis. *Journal of the American Academy of Child & Adolescent Psychiatry, 56*(6), 466–474. https://doi.org/10.1016/j.jaac.2017.03.013

on your race, religion, socioeconomic status, where you live, and what your access to healthcare is like.

This discussion and separation led to autism being gendered as *male autism* or *female autism*. This doesn't sit right with me as it doesn't include people who have the 'opposite gender' autism: non-binary autistics or trans autistics. Ultimately it is also very reductive in how it frames autism; we shouldn't be reduced to A or B kinds of autism because that isn't how autism works; there is so much more diversity than A or B can express.

Instead, I think about this autism binary (if there needs to be one) as internalized autism and externalized autism rather than splitting it by gender. It's not a perfect definition, but, for me at least, it fits with the way that people view autism and our autistic behaviours. What some might have termed male autism I refer to as externalized autism. This is because behaviours are more external and visible to other people. They're things like differences in communication, meltdowns, stimming, and behaviours that fall into the category of observable autistic behaviours. What might have been termed female autism I think of as internalized autism. It aligns with camouflaging/masking, internalizing mental health issues, not being as 'obviously autistic', covert stimming, appearing good at socializing, and not visibly aligning with the stereotypes people associate with autism.

While autism can technically be split into categories that we as autistic people, researchers, or clinicians try to give names to, there is not much benefit in neatly stacking autistic people in different boxes that define and put limits on how we exist. What is, instead, much more helpful is identifying and combating the marginalization, stigmatization, and discrimination that different autistic people experience. We shouldn't just focus on female or male autism but broaden our focus and energy to the discrimination that more marginalized people experience. This includes autistic women, autistic non-binary people, autistic people of colour, and those without financial privilege.

## Diagnosed or self-diagnosed

The simple fact is, you're autistic before you get diagnosed or identified by a clinician. Autism doesn't start when a clinician says you're autistic or writes a diagnostic report stating you are autistic or the specific diagnostic criteria points you meet. Autism is there, within you, throughout your whole life, so whether you self-diagnose or self-identify as autistic, whether you're diagnosed through a publicly or privately funded clinician, or if you never seek a diagnosis, you will always be autistic. Self-diagnosis is just as valid as a clinician's opinion, and it often comes before a clinician decides to make it the kind of official others pay attention to.

This book is for anyone at any point of that identity journey, whether you think you might be autistic or you're sure you are, or you already celebrate your autistic identity, or you're just not sure about any of this yet. Whether anyone explicitly states it or not, the autistic community does and should welcome autistic people whether they've been diagnosed or not. Not everyone is quite there yet, but a lot of us in the autistic community are here to welcome anyone who wishes to explore their autistic identity through self-exploration, self-reflection, and self-diagnosis. Your identity doesn't have to be tied to a diagnosis or a clinician, you can identify as autistic before (or after seeking) a diagnosis. For many, the diagnostic process itself is exclusionary and inaccessible so alternative journeys to autistic acceptance are necessary.

In many countries, publicly funded diagnosis, such as seeking a diagnosis through a publicly funded health system like the NHS in the UK, takes a long time, and there are multiple barriers to accessing diagnosis. These barriers include things like convincing doctors to refer you, the existence of services that can diagnose you, long waiting lists, and having to fit into niche ideas about what autism is or looks like, especially if you don't fit the prescribed stereotypes. For those who have the resources, they may choose a private diagnosis that they, a family member, an employer, an insurance provider, or an education provider may pay for. For some, neither of these public or private routes is feasible, so they don't pursue a diagnosis. Instead, they live knowing for themselves that they are autistic without spending time or money validating their autism.

Beyond this, some autistic people might not know they're autistic. Unless we're afforded the language to describe our experiences and life, we can't explain them using the terms that match what we're trying to say. An example of this has been the meltdowns I've had my entire life (I only learnt about meltdowns aged 21) or the stimming I remember toddler me doing over and over. Suddenly I had the terms to define what was happening to me in those times of distress or times of joyful movement. People may recognize their strengths and differences, but they may not know or recognize these as autistic strengths and differences.

## Is autism a disability?

In society, 'disability' or 'disabled' has been given a negative meaning, both in terms of relating to a person's conditions, illnesses, or impairments and with the general term for 'disabling' something. Disability has historically meant something that is broken, out of action, or not encouraged. This has continued to frame how we think about disability when it is applied to people. Even without realizing it, we're told that disability is terrible by the meaning of the word, but this does not mean that a disability itself is awful. We have the chance to reframe the meaning of words in the way that we use them. If we do not treat disability as a bad word, then it does not have the power to be bad.

The Equality Act (2010) is a piece of British legislation that protects people against discrimination when they have specific protected characteristics. Different countries have different pieces of disability or discrimination legislation. Within the UK's Equality Act, disability is one of these protected characteristics. A disability is defined in the Act as 'a physical or mental impairment that has a "substantial" and "long-term" negative effect on your ability to do normal daily activities'. As autism is substantial, it impacts everything a person does or perceives, and is also long term as it is present throughout someone's whole life. Therefore, autism is considered a disability in this legislation. This Act gives autistic people protection by law to have their rights and needs met.

Disability isn't a terrible label like some definitions might lead us to think, but instead can enable access to support and legal protection. I use the Equality Act definition to explain disability to people in the UK as it uses local political understanding. However, explanations might be different in other countries which have different legislation, or you may prefer to use disability theory models for explaining disability, such as the models of disability explained in the text that follows.

Many people who are autistic consider autism to be a disability; this does not mean that they view being autistic or an autism diagnosis to be negative; you can identify with positive parts of being autistic and the disabling aspects at the same time. Some autistic traits can bring joy, and some can be disabling; it is all dependent on an individual's relationship with their diagnosis and the support they get.

The variety of autistic experiences can mean that the level of disability is also different: some people may not need a lot of support to enable them to live independent lives, whereas others may need significant help to assist them in doing tasks. This is part of why autism is called a spectrum condition.

The argument about whether autism is a disability or not can lead to further debates about the social model of disability and the medical model of disability.[7] In simple terms, the social model of disability means that people are disabled by barriers in society, not by their impairment or condition.

---

7   You can find out more about the social model of disability and the medical model of disability from Scope or Inclusion London.

The medical model describes people as disabled by their impairment or condition, putting the focus on what is 'wrong' with the disabled person rather than what society can do to alleviate barriers to inclusion. Previously autism has been viewed through the medical model lens, but increasingly it is being viewed through the lens of the social model of disability and of neurodiversity. While that does not negate any difficulties that someone has, it puts the onus or responsibility of supporting someone's access or inclusion needs onto society.[8]

People can often get stuck when defining where autism fits into understandings of disability. Autism fits into neurodiversity, it has previously been classed as a mental health condition (it thankfully isn't any more), and someone can identify with autism as a disability. Autism has also been referred to as a 'hidden disability' or 'invisible impairment', which adds another layer of confusion to where autism fits into descriptions of disability.

Sometimes someone identifies as neurodivergent but not as a disabled person; sometimes, people can identify as both. I've always found that by not connecting autism to disability the fact that a neurodivergent person still faces ableism or barriers to accessing the support they need goes unrecognized. Potentially autism doesn't fit neatly into models of disability or even disability itself, but by combining these with neurodiversity, we get a better idea of how autism fits in with the rest of the world.

Truthfully, there aren't simple answers to this question; it all remains a personal preference as to how autistic people individually identify with any of these terms. However, I do wonder what is so bad about calling someone disabled.

---

8   If you are interested in the debates around the social model and what it means for disabled people in general, the work of Mike Oliver, a disabled sociologist and the first professor of disability studies in the UK, makes for a wonderful research rabbit hole. His work will likely leave you feeling ready to become an activist or advocate for disabled people's rights.

## Who is this book for?

This book is intended for autistic teens and young adults (hence the title) but can be read by anyone wanting to know a bit more about autism. You might be questioning whether you are autistic yourself (that's okay to do), reading it because someone you know is autistic, or you may just want to be a better ally to autistic people. The content of the book is most applicable for late teens and young adults but may also be relevant to different ages as things like where you live, employment, education, and healthcare are all critical at any age or stage of life.

If you're an autistic person reading this book, please don't be discouraged if life isn't going the way you want it to or you're at a different place in life when you compare yourself to others. Being autistic and figuring it all out – what autism means for you in your identity, your relationships, what you need for support, and what you want to do with your life – is a big thing to tackle (huge actually) and is lifelong rather than a one-step fix. This book hopes to show you some of the answers, open up more questions, and point you in the direction of finding your place.

So much of my autistic life or life after diagnosis has been figuring myself out and then helping other autistic people figure themselves out in a way that builds them up rather than continuing to break them down. As autistic people, we don't live in a world that naturally understands and accepts us, so we must carve that out for ourselves. This book aims to teach you a bit more about yourself, give you the words to describe your experiences, and help you to have a positive autistic identity.

If you're the parent or family member of an autistic person reading this book, I hope what you can take away is an insight into what autism is like for an autistic person from the perspective of another autistic person. Two things are important here. First is that it is always better to learn about autism from autistic people and to amplify our stories. The second is that this information is general to autism. While I'm drawing upon my knowledge, professional work, and research, you always need to orient your understanding of autism to the personal experiences of specific autistic people like your family member, as not everything will apply to everyone.

If you're non-autistic and reading this book, thank you for taking the time to learn about autism from autistic people. I hope that this book forms part of a journey towards less stigma about autism in broader society. The world isn't always accommodating or supportive of autistic people; what we need to create change is not autistic people pushing for change alone but for non-autistic people to push alongside us.

# Understanding Autism

# What Does Autistic Mean?

An autistic person has differences in how they perceive and interact with their environment, themselves, and those around them. How someone perceives something (takes things in or processes something) may change how they understand the world and what their reaction is. Therefore, autistic people might have behaviours and expressions that are different from non-autistic people. We simply understand the world differently.

Autistic people must display the traits set out in diagnostic criteria to get a diagnosis of autism. If someone doesn't fit the criteria for an autism diagnosis, there might be other diagnoses that are a better fit for their strengths and needs. There are lots of autistic traits that are also part of other conditions that are like autism. Therefore, autistic people and those with attention deficit hyperactivity disorder (ADHD) or other neurodevelopmental conditions might have some similarities. The criteria for an autism diagnosis are outlined in the Diagnostic and Statistical Manual of Mental Disorders (DSM) and the International Classification of Diseases (ICD).[1] The recent

---

1   The DSM is published by the American Psychiatric Association and is predominantly used within the USA to classify mental health conditions. The ICD is maintained by the World Health Organization and is used globally to define health conditions. You might see the DSM called the DSM-5 or DSM-V.

editions, the DSM-5 (2013)[2] and ICD-11 (2018),[3] now have more similar categorizations for autism than they have had in previous editions.[4]

Every autistic person will meet the criteria as laid out in either the DSM-5 or the ICD-11, depending on which country they are diagnosed in. They would have been assessed by a clinician if they sought a formal diagnosis or would have done extensive hours of hyper-focused research if they self-identify as autistic, and importantly they will be unique in what autism means for them. This isn't a linear journey, and some of the steps might be bumpy, but it can describe the course of discovery for each autistic person.

Autistic and autism mean many things to many people. We have the diagnostic frameworks to help us understand autism in a clinical way. We have the words of autistic people to describe autism in our own highly varied ways and the constantly evolving understanding of autism in society. All these different views and ideas have shaped how we think about autism throughout history and up to the present day.

To me, being autistic is my identity. It's not a label that I think of negatively – not any more at least. It's a term that connects me to my community, and through others, I've found a better understanding of myself. It also came with a realization that I'm not bad or broken; that, in fact, I've most often been misunderstood by people who don't understand autism or me. For all of us, being autistic has a personal meaning as well as a broader meaning that others seem to understand (or not). Learning what autism means for you is an integral part of growing an understanding of yourself. You don't always have

2    American Psychiatric Association. (2013). DSM-5 diagnostic classification. *Diagnostic and statistical manual of mental disorders*, 10.
3    World Health Organization. (2018). *International classification of diseases for mortality and morbidity statistics* (11th Revision).
4    Zeldovich, L. (2017). New global diagnostic manual mirrors U.S. autism criteria. Retrieved 29 June 2022, from https://www.spectrumnews.org/news/new-global-diagnostic-manual-mirrors-u-s-autism-criteria

to express your knowledge to others. It can remain a personal journey until you're ready.

## What we have in common

For many autistic people, all we might have in common with another autistic person is our autism diagnosis and a few similarities in autistic traits. Sometimes we are fortunate and share more than just a diagnosis; we find someone with whom we share lots of similarities in what impacts us and what we enjoy. There is nothing more joyful than finding someone else with the same special interests as you, who thinks in the same way as you, who just gets what you are trying to communicate, or has the same stims as you. Finding similarities and differences in the autistic community is something that just feels incredibly different from finding similarities with non-autistic people.

Each autistic person has autistic traits, but the amount that these specific traits can impact on a person's life can vary from person to person and even vary for the same person at different times. When you get an autism diagnosis, the clinician may make you feel like all these autistic differences are things that are wrong with you (if you're lucky they won't do that), but really, they're just your differences that aren't being adequately supported. Some diagnostic reports focus on the things that make you autistic by using a negative framing. Some concentrate on autistic traits in a much more positive way. This can depend on how the clinician works. Ultimately, to get an autism diagnosis, you must show you are different or 'worse' at the diagnostic tasks than a non-autistic person would be, as autism is viewed as a medical or clinical difference from the 'norm'.

This means that an autistic person, just like any person, can have capabilities that fluctuate and change. We can seem 'more' or 'less' autistic depending on the situation and environment around us. No one can be more or less autistic, though; instead, the more or less is generally linked to the visibility of behaviours that are coded as autistic. These visible autistic behaviours might be meltdowns, shutdowns, info-dumping, or awkwardness in social situations.

If someone is comfortable in their environment, they may generally act quite differently from the way they would in an uncomfortable situation. It could be the difference between knowing what to expect and not feeling pressure from a social situation, and being somewhere where there is no structure, no escape, and they may feel they have to perform. It's vital for anyone, autistic or not, to be in situations where they feel happy to be themselves and supported by those around them. Otherwise, this can cause people to mask or camouflage their true selves, which can ultimately be quite damaging. We don't need to be made to feel worse because we're different or feel that we need to hide these differences. We should live our life authentically and be celebrated by those around us.

Some of these difficulties and paths that autistic people tend to experience might resonate with you – we manage similar struggles much as any group that shares characteristics. Every autistic person has similarities and differences that they share with other autistic people, just as non-autistic people are not the same as each other.

## How autism has been defined

Throughout the history of autism, there have been many ways of defining autism and trying to provide meaning to a condition that describes so many different experiences. Autism as a spectrum condition has often been split into categories or ends of the spectrum. Those who have defined these subcategories of autism often seek to differentiate the needs and behavioural presentations of autistic people through our communication, cognitive ability, and social skills to align with how the diagnostic criteria have been sliced up. There have been lots of terms associated with autism to provide meaning to a word that people might not instantly understand when faced with the diversity there is amongst autistic people.

Some of these terms are no longer in use, some have become slurs or insults, and there has been a shift from professionals developing words to define autism to autistic people creating terms to express ourselves.

Autism has been defined as a social communication disorder, developmental disorder, neurodivergence, and a neurodevelopmental condition. From the point autism was first described and classified, the language for defining us has changed dramatically. With the beginnings of the neurodiversity movement and up to the current day's more emancipatory definition led by autistic people, we've pushed for change. The power has shifted, and we as autistic people are able to choose exactly how we want others to describe us and the meanings they associate with us.

These labels can help us to understand the differences that autistic people show between themselves and the differences we have from non-autistic people. Each one brings a slightly different lens through which to understand autism.

## Social communication disorder

This label defines one of the visible differences that autistic people have that other people notice. One of the most 'external' ways that autism is seen by others is through an autistic person's 'performance' in a social situation. As autistic people, we can struggle to talk to or communicate with other people owing to differences in how we communicate that we can't control. Our differences are present in how we communicate with others and how we understand communication.

Autism has also been seen as a disorder or a deficit. However, autism isn't a medical condition like many other illnesses that are given a disorder label. Autism can be called a condition, as it is a condition that affects how you see the world. For some autistic people, communicating with others is the thing about being autistic that impacts them the most.

This label for autism highlights how autism has been viewed and categorized through a medical lens. Autism is considered to share some of the facets of social communication disorder, but they are seen as separate diagnoses. A social communication disorder isn't a difficulty with speech (pronouncing words or putting sentences together) but is a difficulty with the pragmatic aspects of communication like social rules. Before there were more options on job applications I would normally tick 'social communication disorder' or 'learning difficulty' as I never really knew how autism fitted in and they were the closest correct-enough options for me.

## Developmental disorder

Some autistic people might develop at a slower or faster rate than non-autistic people, meeting developmental milestones at different times or inconsistently. This can be in lots of different areas of life. Some people are slower at learning in school, others might be delayed in their speech or language, some might struggle with their movement or coordination, and autistic people may vary in their social skills.

For those who also have a learning disability, physical health condition, or learning difficulty, it might be more evident that they have a delay in an area of their development related to their co-occurring conditions. For others, it might not be as apparent until they get a bit older. We generally associate the word development with infancy and childhood, but some parts of development continue for decades into our lives. We might not know what our developmental differences are until later in life, and those around us might only realize how different we were growing up once we get to look back. Things are often easiest to reflect on with hindsight.

The term developmental disorder also reminds us that autism is something you have your whole life, even before someone diagnoses you. Autistic children grow up into autistic adults whose needs change and develop as they age. This goes against the previous terminology, which included the label 'childhood autism' as if autism is something that magically evaporates on your 18th birthday.

## Neurodivergence and neurodiversity

The term neurodiversity was popularized by sociologist Judy Singer in the late 1990s.[5] Neurodiversity is a term used to describe the natural differences and variations between people's brains (*neuro-* being the brain and *-diversity* being difference) and how they think. As a way of describing the entire range of natural differences in human cognition, neurodiversity ranges from neurodivergent to neurotypical.

Neurodiversity is genuinely infinite in the differences that can happen in the human brain and does not mean that something is wrong with someone's brain. Neurodivergence includes developmental differences and conditions that relate to the brain, such as autism, dyspraxia, dyslexia, dyscalculia, ADHD, Tourette's, and other differences in a person's brain. Neurotypical simply means anyone who is not neurodivergent. While this might be most people (the neuromajority), this does not make being neurotypical better or worse than being neurodivergent. I sometimes find it simpler to use non-autistic rather than neurotypical if I know the person is not autistic as you never know what diagnosis someone might have or if they are pre-diagnosis.

Neurodiversity focuses on the differences between people's brains rather than what historically may have been termed deficits. The focus on differences does not eliminate or lessen the exclusion and ableism that neurodivergent people experience. As an example, while someone with ADHD may have difficulty with time management or differences in their ability to focus on one or multiple tasks, they also may have strengths in their creativity, their approach to solving problems, or greater interest in the things that they find joy in. The things that someone excels at do not negate the things that trip them up – we still have support needs alongside struggles in other

---

5   Singer, J. (1998). *Odd people in: The birth of community amongst people on the autistic spectrum: A personal exploration of a new social movement based on neurological diversity.* Sydney: Faculty of Humanities and Social Science, University of Technology Sydney.

areas. For an autistic person, this might mean they should try not to view sensory differences as deficits, but instead, see these differences as an alternative way of experiencing the world or highlighting strengths that others do not see.

In terms of the language around neurodiversity, a group can be neurodiverse, but a person is not neurodiverse. A person is either neurodivergent or neurotypical. Neurodivergent people should be recognized and respected for their differences, and these differences should not be viewed as things that make them lesser or worse than neurotypical people. Often neurodivergence and the differences that we have from neurotypicals are wrongfully stigmatized by society. Instead of blaming neurodivergent people for our differences, the environment can and should be blamed for not being supportive enough of our needs. This is because we exist in a society and a world that isn't built with us in mind. Instead, the world is constructed in tangible and intangible ways to only work for neurotypical people and, more unfortunately still, made to work well for a small percentage of neurotypical people.

While society might tell us that we are wrong or bad for being neurodivergent (they're wrong about that), there are some areas where neurodivergent people excel. Some areas of strength that neurodivergent people may have are:

- differences in thinking style or problem-solving
- looking at the finer or smaller details rather than the bigger picture
- a more profound way of thinking
- intense concentration (particularly on things of personal joy and interest, also termed hyperfocus)
- a strong sense of honesty, justice, and loyalty.

Sadly, some of these strengths are thought of as weaknesses, which they honestly aren't. These are just differences from the norm that society isn't built to favour. These skills and differences often mean that as neurodivergent people, we might be seen as thinking outside the box, bringing fresh perspectives to problem-solving, or being a disruptor. Those are all incredible skills to have, but our skills are a bit of a square peg trying to fit into a round hole; we're not made to fit in, and we shouldn't have to.

Strengths like these in a system that isn't built to support them can mean that neurodivergent people are often seen as having rather spiky profiles with strengths and successes in some areas of life but facing more difficulty in others. An example of this is potentially doing poorly in school because of the exam-focused way of assessing learning. Although, you may perform well at work if given the opportunity to work on a project or topic in an area that you find interesting with a workload and assessment model that matches your strengths. For some this might be a memory-based exam; for others, it is practical tasks; and for yet others, it is assessments in lots of small chunks – nothing works for everyone.

This variability from person to person and within the same person but in different situations can make both strengths and weaknesses appear more pronounced, so while you might shine at some things, you might appear absolutely rubbish at others. For me, this means I can verbally articulate my ideas well, but this never translated to my essays. So instead, to utilize my strengths rather than the weaknesses that different formats highlighted, I verbally present my ideas rather than use written forms – it has made writing a book very interesting. Sometimes I'd use dictation to turn my thoughts into words on a page. Having strengths in certain areas and weaknesses in others doesn't mean you're stuck like that. It means you might need a bit of time to figure out what support you need or what ways of working allow you to shine.

Neurodiversity is a positive way of looking at autism. This might be because the idea was popularized by Judy Singer, who is neurodivergent herself. There are strengths in language about us being chosen and shaped by us. When viewed alongside the social model of disability, neurodiversity makes sense, at least on the surface. It can get a bit tricky when you dig down more deeply into it, but no theory is perfect. There is nothing wrong with us as disabled, autistic, or neurodivergent people. It is society that needs to change to support us. Society is the thing that fails to include us.

If you would like to learn more about neurodiversity, I would strongly recommend reading more of Judy Singer's work on neurodiversity or reading more contemporary works like *The Neurodiversity Reader*, a collection of writing by neurodivergent academics edited by Damian Milton. Some writing can be difficult to engage with around neurodiversity as it is often written by academics or for employers, but there are more accessible texts and formats out there.

### Neurodevelopmental condition

Neurodevelopmental condition is a phrase that can be broken down into its component parts.

Neuro means the brain, and as the brain controls everything, that means autism impacts and interacts with everything an autistic person does. Autism is in every aspect of our brains, our thoughts, our experiences, our acts, and our feelings, and is in every molecule of our body. It is probably in every molecule – I'm not that kind of researcher or scientist, so people who understand biology, genetics, or the human body better than me might disagree with me here. Research has shown some brain differences in autistic people, from how our brain is structured, to how it interconnects, to how it reacts to different body chemicals.

Developmental means it is there from the earliest stages of development; autism is something you're born with and not something you can cure, and it continues throughout your entire life. Although someone is autistic before they are even born, it isn't something that can be diagnosed until later. Diagnosis often comes once someone has noticed the behaviours that are linked to being autistic, as we haven't figured out the other ways of 'detecting' autism yet. Although to be very bluntly honest, I'm not sure I'd like a screening tool or test to be devised as the only eventuality I can envision from that is the removal of autistic people.

Autism is recognized through behavioural observation at any point in someone's development. Some research indicates that autism can be observed from the age of 12 months old; the reliability of these observations and ideas improves from 18 months old. Clinicians have done extensive amounts of research to try to figure out the differences we have and when we start showing them, but their research into our developmental differences isn't perfect as some people are never diagnosed, and many are diagnosed late in life.

Condition is used to describe autism more than disorder as it is a more positive way of thinking about autism that holds less stigma. By using condition instead of disorder, there isn't the negativity or the medical connotations that you might get with the word disorder or disease because autism isn't a disease. It is a way of thinking, being, and doing.

The world uses lots of terms to describe autism – some can be incredibly negative, and some can be empowering. It is up to each autistic person to choose how they want to be defined. You don't have to accept definitions of yourself that make you feel bad about yourself. By learning from how autism has been and is currently explained, we can better figure out how we fit in. There is, as I will always say, an inherent power in language, and having the language that feels right to you to describe yourself is one of the most powerful things about exploring autism.

## Our autistic differences

To help understand what makes an autistic person different from a non-autistic person, we can categorize these differences into four distinct areas:

1. communication
2. interaction

3. processing
4. sensory.

Some of these words and differences might resonate with you, or you might find more of yourself in other ways of describing autism. How you define yourself is entirely up to you. These differences aren't wrong, they don't make a person less than or worse than another person, and they aren't curable. They are just a person's particular way of doing something. These differences don't align perfectly with the autism diagnostic criteria but are how I describe autism to others without using jargon or confusing words.

## Communication
The first difference that autistic people have from our non-autistic peers is in communication. Communication, simply put, is when you talk to another person, you listen to what they are saying, look at the actions they make with their face and body, and think of what to say in response. Communication is both receptive (what we receive from others) and expressive (what we share with others). As autistic people, we can have differences or imbalances in both our receptive and expressive communication.

Autistic people struggle to juggle many tiny parts of communication at the same time, so we might communicate using different words, sounds, or gestures to what people might expect. People generally communicate in a wide variety of ways depending on the social situation that they are in. We don't talk to children in the same way that we speak to authority figures, for example. Communication happens in the way we move our hands, our bodies, our eyes, our face, and our mouths. Everything we say and do communicates messages big and small to those we directly choose to share with and even those we don't.

Everything a person does around others can be seen and interpreted as communicating a point that might match what they are trying to convey. This is where, as autistic people, we are commonly thought to have trouble with understanding others' communication or present differently in how we communicate when compared with a non-autistic person. As autistic people, we understand the world around us differently, and that means that an autistic perception of what someone is saying, how they are saying it, and the implicit messages might be different to the intended message, concept, or idea. It's the same for non-autistic people's interpretation of what an autistic person might mean. The misunderstanding goes both ways.[6]

Sometimes you might hear someone say that autistic people prefer explicit communication, things to be clear or concrete, or just for any vagueness that might be in language to be removed. This could be by others not using metaphors, sarcasm, idioms, or allegorical language that don't directly mean what they are meant to. Having said that, some of the most sarcastic and witty people I know are autistic, so differences and difficulties don't apply in the same way to everyone. These things (idioms, analogies, and metaphors) can be learnt, but it doesn't help that the words aren't being used literally. In these cases, understanding comes from a shared knowledge of what the words you're using in that sentence, in that exact order, mean. An example of this is the question 'How far away is our next meeting?' This could be interpreted in several ways, and the speaker is relying on listeners putting the question in context and intuiting which way is intended.

'How far away is our next meeting?'

Without context, we might think this person is talking about

---

6    If you want to read up on this autistic/non-autistic miscommunication, often referred to as the 'double empathy problem', I suggest the work of autistic academic Dr Damian Milton, who originally conceived the term. The double empathy problem outlines that people with different world/life experiences will struggle to empathize with each other, something only made more profound by communication differences like the ones autistic people have.

the distance or the location of the next meeting, as 'far away' is typically used to talk about distance. However, they could be intending to mean 'when' rather than 'where', thinking about the days, weeks, or months between the current meeting and the next. We don't know the context unless we ask, and often we don't feel able to ask for context to confirm the meaning. We must rely on people's intonation, their emphasis on specific words, and the context. That's a lot to balance and juggle when you think about it.

Something I've always been told is that I'm incredibly articulate and clear. I'm able to describe accurately what I'm trying to convey and match my communication style to that of my conversation partner so that I am understood. This is part of what hid my autism throughout my childhood and adolescence. I read so many books that I stuffed myself full of phrases and language. My communication relies incredibly heavily on my being highly observant, reflective, and able to process what is going on, something that has taken a lot of years, a lot of skill, and a lot of energy to build up. I purposefully build in processing buffers with body language (I use my hands a lot), filling sentences and describing around my point so that others are perfectly clear on what message I'm sharing. Yet even so I frequently end any monologue or explanation with 'I hope that made sense'.

For you, it might be different. You might be good at understanding what others are saying and feel that you are constantly misunderstood by others no matter how you try to get your point across. We're all different in how we communicate with others and have different struggles or strengths. What is fundamental is finding out what your skills are and making use of them.

### Interaction

Interaction covers all the aspects of our social behaviour, and the social rules people are expected to use when interacting with each other. Often these rules aren't always used in the same way in different situations, and the patterns of everyone's social behaviour are intricately woven together in such a way as to be almost incomprehensible. At the very least, it is intended to be incomprehensible to autistic people. Interacting with others is something that should be easy. We can observe all these social rules by just watching others and learning what they mean, but it is often much more complex as the social cues can be incredibly subtle or used to tell a lie.

If you're autistic, this might mean differences in how you understand and put in place social rules you've seen and learnt throughout your lifetime. Some of them make sense, and a lot more of the social rules in the world don't. I learnt about social rules for interacting with others by watching films, TV programmes, reading books, watching other people interact, and figuring things out by making a bunch of mistakes I could have done without. The problem with these sources of learning how to socialize is that some of them are highly stylized, create more drama, and don't correctly reflect real life. I mean, no one gets to listen to their inner voice for extended periods of time during a conversation like they do on film or in TV programmes (I'm looking at you *Scrubs*).

We know that social rules and social niceties are constructed because they are different in different cultures. A specific body language movement in one country that shows enjoyment might be considered deeply offensive in another country. These rules work in one country or culture but don't translate. What is weirder still is that sometimes social rules don't mean the same or aren't adhered to equally in the same country or culture. In villages, people are potentially much more friendly and hospitable, but in big cities, people sometimes aren't as nice or friendly to strangers or people they've just met. Walking a street in a busy town, you're much more likely to avoid eye contact with anyone and move as quickly as possible to fit in with the flow of 'people traffic' rather than the slightly slower pace of rural living.

For a non-autistic person picking up on these social rules

and the innate way that society works appears much more straightforward than for an autistic person, who often must learn through trial and error what to do in a social situation. This means that we create scripts and run-throughs of what social situations entail and what interactions demand of us, and to outsiders, it might appear robotic or as if we are working through a fixed pattern. However, if you only know one routine that works, you will use a reliable pattern of interacting with others. These are things like practising your coffee order, rehearsing what to say at family gatherings, preparing for medical appointments, or just having set topics of conversation you feel comfortable with.

Things like masking or camouflaging are now much more understood as a part of autistic interactions in a neurotypical world. Masking is the practice of socially compensating[7] for autistic interaction and communication differences by performing in social situations with the hope of hiding or shielding the ways that we might struggle during social interactions. We attempt to seem as neurotypical as possible to protect our autistic identity by hiding differences or changing the way we naturally act in a social situation. We often do this because being openly autistic isn't always safe in every situation, and it can seem easier to reflect neurotypical social skills in neurotypical social situations.[8] It takes a lot out of us to invest the time and energy needed to try to 'pass' as neurotypical.

---

7   In research, masking, camouflaging, and social compensation are all terms that are given to this complex web of strategies and actions that autistic people take to reduce the outward appearance of autistic behaviours to fit in. You might use one or all these terms, but I've found masking is the one that fits best –both as a hypothetical mask it feels like I hold up and the very real ways in which I mask my naturally autistic actions.

8   If you want to read more about this, there is a research paper that helped form my perspectives on masking (and developed it into a special interest) by Laura Hull and colleagues (2017). The research is available to be read by anyone and focuses on the perspectives of autistic people about masking and what the consequences are. If you prefer a graphic novel style *Camouflage* (2019) by Dr Sarah Bargiela combines descriptive illustrations by Sophie Standing and accessible writing.

In social situations with autistic people, we might find it easier to interact with each other because we already have that mutual understanding that is often missing when we interact with non-autistic people. Just as non-autistic people have their social rules, there are autistic social rules and norms. They're just not as strict because we understand each other's differences and difficulties.

## Processing

Ultimately autistic people think differently and process things differently from non-autistic people. That's a simple fact. Our brains are different by design and so have an indisputable difference to a non-autistic brain. Research is available that shows our brain differences, but I was never quite good enough at neuroscience to decode any of it. You'd have to ask a neuroscientist what the differences are.

Remember, difference does not mean bad, wrong, or deficient. Difference can be an entirely neutral word when we let it be. Our processing differences are split into categories that help us understand these differences:

*Executive function*, or rather executive dysfunction, means autistic people are not always great with things that involve planning, goals, remembering to do something, or organizing ourselves or our time. It completely changes how we approach tasks and the support we need to complete them. Our executive function differences also mean that we might not be able to manage change easily, complex processes can be challenging to follow, and we have difficulties with memory and the emotions connected with planning and doing (especially if things don't go right). This is dependent on a part of memory called working memory, which is essentially the part of memory that juggles all the tasks, facts, and things you need to remember to do. For autistic people, executive function or working memory is like juggling with hard mode constantly enabled.

*Information processing* is a bit of a mixed situation. We might be better at processing specific types of information and much worse at processing others. We might be bad at emotional processing and better at analysing logical situations. We might be faster at problem-solving but much slower to process the things that we struggle with. For me, processing emotions is never something I can do at the time, and it can take me days, weeks, months, or even years to figure out what my emotions are or mean. On the other hand, I feel like a highly qualified spy with my ability to dissect complex information quickly, process the information, and figure out what it means. If the information isn't about my feelings, I'm speedy at processing it, my brain makes logical leaps well, and emotions don't feel like logic to me.

*Understanding phrases* is something we might not always be able to do. The English language is packed with idioms that are used to share tacit meaning. When things have both a literal meaning and a figurative meaning, we can struggle as we might think of the literal meaning first and be unable to disengage from it. Phrases like 'the elephant in the room' don't mean a literal elephant squeezed into a room but instead the figurative meaning is intended – something people know about but are avoiding. Some phrases don't necessarily make sense, but once you learn them, you can understand the meaning people intend. Although really, I'd rather that people were straightforward and clear to begin with; that would make everything much easier than having to have a mental catalogue of 'they don't actually mean this, they mean that'.

*Planning for the future* is something we can really struggle with. We might struggle with planning for the future if we don't have a script or understanding of how to undertake a task. We might also struggle with the future, particularly if it changes unexpectedly and no longer matches the plan we have internally. We can be both internally paralysed by the idea of making plans and hurt by plans changing, even if we haven't told someone what our plans are. Reconciling expectations and reality can be difficult, so for things like this I find it best to communicate my expectations as clearly as possible to help manifest and shape my reality – it doesn't always work but it helps.

*Sharing perspectives* with others is something described as a Theory of Mind, empathy, and a bunch of other phrases that try to describe the differences in how autistic and non-autistic people view the world. Our differences in Theory of Mind are an area of research that has been explored for decades and it is generally suggested that autistic people are worse than non-autistic people at this type of perspective sharing. On the whole, I think the double empathy problem is better at describing this difference in a way that doesn't feel like a deficit but more like a mismatch. We think differently and may not always hold the same perspective as others. Many have said that autistic people 'can't see the forest for the trees', which as an idiom means we focus on the detail and not the bigger picture, we often get lost in focusing on smaller things. We don't fit as well into conventional thinking as others would wish, mainly because we are typically unconventional and out-of-the-box thinkers, which is a strength when it is harnessed but not when it is ostracized.

Our information-processing skills are much better described as working from the catalogue of experiences we've built. They aren't innate. We can build our catalogue of experiences by experiencing things (even if they're scary), using similar experiences to inform us, or by watching the world around us either through films or our personal experiences. To understand and interact with the world, we try to use our 'most correct/least bad' way of doing something from the ways that we have learnt to do them.

We all process information in different ways and have different routes to arrive at the same answer or place. For autistic people, this can be a different way of thinking, needing a little longer to think, remembering information that doesn't seem connected to what is currently being discussed, or reacting to the information in a way that someone doesn't expect.

## Sensory

The world is made up of so many ways to experience it, and as autistic people, we can have differences in how we experience, understand, process, and interact with the world. For some autistic people, the world can feel like every sense is turned up in sensitivity so that sensory experiences can feel overwhelming or painful. For others, it might be that they don't get enough information from the world around them, so they seek it out as these senses aren't painful but rather enjoyable. It can feel a bit like everything is either dialled up or muted; we don't get to experience things in their full range, and we often oscillate between extremes.

The senses go beyond the five we're taught about (sight, sound, taste, touch, and smell) to include things like our vestibular, proprioception, and interoception senses. Our vestibular sense is the awareness of how we move our bodies or our balance, proprioception is our awareness of where our body parts are even when we can't see them, and interoception is our awareness of what is going on inside of us. We're constantly assessing and reassessing through these senses.

There is a whole lot more than our body is aware of that we may even be able to process ourselves. With all our eight senses constantly receiving information at once, we are made to process what feels like a never-ending stream of information, figure out what it means, and react to it. For some of us autistic people, this can be unbelievably overwhelming due to being hypersensitive to the sensory world, and for others, we might be under-sensitive to certain senses. We can be highly sensory seeking, prone to searching for sensory experiences that we enjoy or want to experience, or we can be sensory aversive, trying our hardest to avoid the experiences that we just don't want to feel. For me, this presents as enjoying soft fabrics or objects with repeating tactile patterns but avoiding things that are overly loud and overwhelming.

Autistic people may struggle with processing these senses as other people might understand them or may even use their senses in ways that others might not expect. Someone may use their experience of their senses to show their emotions.

Some autistic people might stimulate their senses in response to their feelings in a way that is individual to them. This is something called self-stimulatory behaviour or 'stimming'. Some people might stim when they are anxious, to show they're happy, or to help manage anger. Stimming[9] is the repetitive body movement or sound made by an autistic person that stimulates their senses. It's not done for other people or to annoy anyone else. It's entirely for us.

## Diagnosis and finding your community

Diagnosis can feel like the end of an arduous process or the start of a lifelong lesson in understanding yourself, or both. For autistic people, the route to diagnosis is rarely easy. For many of us, it can come at the end of a series of immense struggles. These struggles can be in education, through a mental health crisis, being bullied by others, a traumatic life change, or if you were pretty young when you were diagnosed, then the struggle might be something your family went through that you may not remember fully. A positive diagnosis can be a very odd experience for some. It can either confirm what you've researched and reassured yourself about, or can feel completely unexpected.

Everyone has their own unique experience of receiving their autism diagnosis. It's something that can be tinged with so much happiness and so much sadness all at the same time. For me, it came right at the point where I had been struggling for so long, I had lost all sense of positive self-esteem, and I was convinced there was something entirely, utterly, and catastrophically wrong with me. I mean, why else would people

---

9    I go into more detail on stimming later, so don't worry if this doesn't feel like enough depth just yet! There is more on stimming in the 'Strengths, differences, and challenges' chapter and a quick description in the Glossary.

have bullied me for so long and so viciously? Why else would my brain betray me by telling me I was worthless? Why else would I feel so overwhelmed the whole time, feeling like I'm drowning and utterly incapable of swimming?[10] Why else would I struggle so much to make and keep friends who like me?

That's not to say that diagnosis is guaranteed to make any of this better. For me, it was three hours of diving into everything I'm absolutely terrible at and feeling so judged for everything that had been entirely normal for me for my entire life. I was evaluated for what I can do well and the things I'm not great at, all measured using an autism assessment made for children as I only just fitted the criteria for child and adolescent diagnostic services.

There are two points to make here. First, I'm very good at the things I'm good at and not great at the things I struggle with. Being made to focus on the things I couldn't do, and the things that people had mocked me for my entire life wasn't the best way to build a positive identity around autism. It felt like a traumatic deep dive through what had not gone well up to this point. Second, playing with toys and playing pretend felt like a bizarre way to diagnose my autism. This is mainly because I was an 18-year-old when I was assessed. It felt ridiculous playing with toys, creating a story, and reading the terrible book about frogs, all while talking about the undeniable signs I was autistic as a young child.

Autism was the correct answer to a question I had never asked. What hurt most was why it took so long for someone to ask what felt like the most obvious question. All the answers had been right there my entire life.

I mean, why else would I only go to school discos if I could cover my ears and face away from the lights? It even got to the point where I described myself as allergic to strobe lights – completely normal behaviour of course! Swimming lessons

---

10   Ironically, I can't swim, so I would drown in almost any situation involving lots of water, but we'll ignore that for this metaphor.

caused me so much sensory overload that I always stayed in the shallow end of the pool and struggled through classes until they ended. What I, as a child, did not realize at the time is that I'm not very good at learning very practical things like swimming or driving from someone talking me through it.[11] My muscles need to know what my brain might technically understand.

All the assessments made me realize that I really did do a lot of things wrong. All the signs were right there, but nobody was looking at me for long enough or kindly enough to recognize them. At the end of the assessment, they brought my mum and me back together, both of us exhausted by three hours of talking and being observed for the meaning behind our every word and movement. They told us to wait for the post and showed us which button to press to release the door when leaving. Bare your entire soul, now off you pop, next please!

Six weeks later I got the thick wedge of my diagnostic report through the post. Six pages affirming that I'm autistic and detailing my failings and the things I would struggle with for the rest of my life. It's so weird to see your life summarized by a near stranger casting a clinical lens on every little memory and thought you shared. For a time, it made me much more guarded about how I shared myself with others and caused me to hold shame about my autistic identity. I sought ways to lessen myself and make my autism small, unobtrusive, and inoffensive for others.

The 2014, freshly diagnosed version of myself is not something I'm proud of in the slightest. For me diagnosis was not liberation – it built walls of internalized ableism that I'm still battling to break down. It wasn't a positive experience until I found support and solidarity in the autistic community.

That's the thing that changed everything for me. Finding my people. I didn't find myself suddenly surrounded by autistic people in real life after my diagnosis; I worked to create

---

11  A side note to this: I've been diagnosed as dyspraxic while writing this book, so this probably also had something to do with not grasping physical skills well!

a connection to my community. I began volunteering with my local autism charity, meeting autistic children and young people through my volunteering, seeing what autism looked like in other people, and finding my community online. Many people say that the autistic community thrives online, socializing is technically easier, and we can often find each other in the spaces where we can talk about our special interests. It was on Tumblr and, later, Twitter that I was able to find out more about autism from autistic people themselves and form friendships with autistic people with so many experiences both different and alike to my own. Stumbling upon #ActuallyAutistic at a time when I was quite isolated from other autistic people was the perfect salve for the metaphorical wound in my life left by the words of diagnosing clinicians and cruel peers.

I can't emphasize enough just how important it is to find yourself a community to support you, to lift you back up, and to rely on when things get hard. Oddly, realizing I wasn't weird or special because there were and are so many people out there who are exactly like me, did absolute wonders for my self-esteem. I was no longer a snowflake once I found myself in a snowstorm.

# Myths and Stereotypes about Autism

As an autistic person, there are many stereotypes you will hear or see about autism. In film, media, writing, and the world around you, there are a lot of misconceptions about what autism is. This is partially due to what the medical and societal understanding of autism has historically been and how it has grown over the decades since work about autism was first theorized and publicized. Autism has been described by researchers, professionals, parents of autistic people, people with no connection to autism, and autistic people themselves. When there are so many different views being shared, this can create some misinformation and misunderstanding about what autism is and what it isn't.

One of the first films focused on autism that gained widespread public attention was *Rain Man*. The film created an idea of autism from the viewpoints of professionals, family members, and the general public rather than from autistic perspectives. The cultural impact of *Rain Man* has shaped what people understand about autism, learning disabilities, and savant syndrome, but it doesn't accurately reflect what autistic people are like or tell the stories we want to tell from our perspectives. *Rain Man* tells a specific story from a specific viewpoint and because of this it can't be generalized to all autistic people, but it did ensure that the word autism, or at the very least savantism, became known.

Since the release of *Rain Man* in 1988, the understanding and conceptualization of autism have grown exponentially. Unfortunately, many portrayals of autism in film and media follow in the storytelling footprints of *Rain Man*, focusing on the 'deficits' that autistic people have, the 'burden' we are on others, and creating a very specific picture of what an autistic person looks like and how they behave.

## What is a myth?

A myth is a traditional story to explain natural or social phenomena. This type of storytelling is used in many cultures and societies to explain their beliefs, thoughts, and past deeds. Unfortunately, while a myth can be a legend of history or previous cultures, it can also be a widely held but false belief or idea. While a myth might have cultural worth to tell the tales of lives in the past, it does not tell the whole truth; instead, it mixes elements of truth with embellishments.

For autism this means there are myths created as a result of the way autism has been perceived through history, taking potential truths or half-truths and twisting them into the cultural understanding of autism. Not all myths are good, and some need to be challenged.

## What is a stereotype?

Stereotypes are widely held beliefs about people or objects that are often too fixed and oversimplified. A stereotype might simplify an idea to the point of it being incorrect or only correct in very few cases. Frequently, a stereotype might be the idea that someone holds when presented with a concept to help them think about what something might include or entail. It focuses on the 'standard' or 'conventional' view of something and describes this at face value or based on initial impressions. A stereotype is often confronted and challenged when someone learns more about the person or object in question.

Applying a stereotype to a whole group of people can cause harm to those who don't fit within that narrow viewpoint.

Myths and stereotypes about autism come from how it has been understood, researched, and published throughout history and up to the present day. Some myths and stereotypes have built up over time and others grow quickly. Every preconception about autism has some basis in ideas created by society, so while it might not be completely accurate or reflective of autistic people, there may be some truth at the root of it.

## Myths about who can be autistic and what they look like

### Myth: autism is something that people grow out of

Although historically autism has been described as 'childhood schizophrenia' and 'childhood autism', it is not something that impacts someone only in childhood. Often autism is diagnosed when someone is young and services to support them are focused on this age range. Autism is most visible in childhood and education as that is currently where most of the support is focused. Support in education (and any other setting) gives autistic people some of the confidence and skills to know how to support themselves and manage the world around them. While there is support in education for those who have a diagnosis and whose needs have been identified, this does not mean that everyone gets the support that they need or that those not diagnosed until adulthood don't need support.

The 'truth' that this myth relies on is that autism might be less obvious as someone grows older. Difference is something that is much more noticeable in a classroom of people the same age as you, but far less noticeable when you can choose the space you're in. As autistic young people and adults, we have a bit of autonomy or choice about the spaces we spend time in. Often these are spaces that make us happy. We can choose to get jobs in areas we are passionate about, spend time on hobbies where we can pursue our special interests, and socialize in the ways that work best for us.

All these things hide autism in plain sight; we aren't less autistic, we're just in places where our differences aren't seen as a difference but as a strength. This also unfortunately highlights that autism is most easily seen when someone is in crisis or has been through trauma; people find it much harder to 'see' us when we aren't traumatized. We become hidden in adulthood when the coping mechanisms that we've developed shield the difficulties we're compensating for or managing.

For many autistic people, the way autism impacts them changes during their lifetime; we may face challenges at different points of our life that might not be seen by the world around us. There are more services and support for us during the earlier years of our life, less in the middle, and then more when we get older, but they're not always inclusive of our needs. Instead of only focusing on getting things right from the start (which isn't always right or at the start), what we need is support throughout our lives to help reduce the challenges and celebrate more of the successes.

It feels like a radical thought, but what autistic people really need is inclusive, personalized, and lifelong support alongside people realizing that autism is a lifelong condition. Adding onto that, coping mechanisms that help at one point in our lives may not apply to every other part of our lives or to every situation we face.

### Myth and stereotype: autistic people are white, middle-class boys

This myth connects with the history of autism, particularly due to Leo Kanner's original study of autism, which has a small sample of mainly white boys (eight boys and three girls) who lived in and around Baltimore, Maryland.[1] Although it is not

---

1   Kanner, L. (1943). Autistic disturbances of affective contact. *Nervous Child*, 2(3), 217–250.

a myth that those initially diagnosed by Kanner were white and generally male with certain levels of privilege in their life, it has developed into both a myth and a stereotype that has both positively and negatively impacted autistic people. The positive impacts have been felt by those who are like those initially examined by Kanner, but it hasn't helped those who don't match this narrow exploration of autism.

When you think about autism and its representation in the media, people most often think of white boys and men who have a certain level of privilege that enabled them to get diagnosed at a young age. It evokes ideas of Sheldon Cooper from *The Big Bang Theory*, Raymond Babbitt from *Rain Man*, Dr Shaun Murphy from *The Good Doctor*, Joe Hughes from *The A Word*, or Sam Gardner from *Atypical*. Having this sort of representation of autism in the science that has defined us and media portrayals that describe us means that for those who don't fit this neat stereotype it can be much more difficult to access a diagnosis and support. Instead, those who don't fit this idea, those who 'don't look autistic', might have to endure additional stigma and potentially be misdiagnosed as their autistic presentation is misunderstood.

Things are now changing in research, media, and wider society when it comes to autism, gender, age, race, and social circumstance. Research has broadened much more to include an increased focus on autistic people who don't fit this stereotype. More women are being diagnosed, more autistic people of colour are being diagnosed, more trans and non-binary people are being diagnosed, and the effects of uneven privilege in accessing diagnosis more quickly are better understood now.

### Myth: autistic people have no empathy

Empathy is defined as being able to understand other people's thoughts and feelings. Sympathy is understanding the feelings of others from your perspective. The difference between empathy and sympathy is where you situate yourself. For sympathy, it is from your perspective, and for empathy, you try to understand the situation from another person's perspective. Empathy and autism have been explored and researched over the decades, resulting in several different theories:

- Theory of Mind (1985)[2]
- mindblindness (1997)[3]
- empathizing–systemizing theory (2002)[4]
- the double empathy problem (2012).[5]

This is a myth that has its roots in a scientific theory about autism and some of the stereotypes that have developed from it. A researcher based at the University of Cambridge, Simon Baron-Cohen, developed a theory of explaining autistic differences from non-autistic people through two variables: empathizing and systemizing. His theory describes the idea that autistic people have below-average empathy and average or above-average systemizing skills. The separate empathy and systemizing skills are used together to categorize people into one of the five different brain types that Baron-Cohen has defined. Autistic people are labelled as poor at empathizing and good at systemizing according to this theory, but this isn't always the case as not all autistic people are exactly alike – all we generally share is a diagnosis.

This empathizing–systemizing theory also fits with the previous myth about autism and boys or men as Simon Baron-Cohen further developed his theory into 'extreme male brain theory'. He and his colleagues found that those

2   Baron-Cohen, S., Leslie, A. M., & Frith, U. (1985). Does the autistic child have a 'theory of mind'? *Cognition, 21*(1), 37–46. https://doi.org/10.1016/0010-0277(85)90022-8

3   Baron-Cohen, S. (1997). *Mindblindness: An essay on autism and theory of mind.* MIT Press.

4   Baron-Cohen, S. (2002). The extreme male brain theory of autism. *Trends in Cognitive Sciences, 6*(6), 248–254. https://doi.org/10.1016/S1364-6613(02)01904-6

5   Milton, D. E. (2012). On the ontological status of autism: the 'double empathy problem'. *Disability & Society, 27*(6), 883–887. https://doi.org/10.1080/09687599.2012.710008

who scored higher as systemizers and lower as empathizers were generally male and the opposite was true for females.

In its simplest understanding, this theory can be taken to mean that autistic people either have no empathy or low empathy. This harmful idea matched with autistic people's atypical way of expressing empathy has meant that people do believe that we can't empathize with people or situations. We're more likely to empathize in a different way to what people expect, at different times, and in different situations. A lot of this misunderstanding is based on people having expectations of autistic people that don't match the reality of how we act, think, feel, or express ourselves.

For example, our empathetic response might be that we're more pragmatic or problem- and solutions-focused rather than showing our internal feelings externally. A lot of autistic people are said to have 'flat affect', which means that we don't always show our emotions on our faces, so why would we suddenly start when others' expectations of empathy demand smiles or frowns? More often than not I might be really enjoying something, but you wouldn't be able to tell by looking at my face, which generally just has an expression somewhere on the spectrum from resting bitch face to squinting because of my astigmatism.

So, autistic people might express their empathy differently to non-autistic people; we might not use platitudes, instead focusing on practical ways to move forward, or we might chat someone through something, verbally consoling them rather than physically consoling them with a hug. However, you might behave completely differently: not every autistic person is alike and we all experience empathy in different ways! That's the whole point: while I could endlessly describe ways of experiencing empathy, I don't know how you empathize with others.

Really, the idea that autistic people don't have empathy could not be further from the truth. Autistic people can experience the whole spectrum of empathy from hypo-empathy (low empathy) to hyper-empathy (high empathy). These aren't static states. Being high or low in empathy is not a bad thing; often people confuse empathy with sympathy or compassion but they're not the same. Being high or low in empathy does not mean that someone does or doesn't care. Empathy doesn't make someone a good or bad person; it relates more to how they respond to a situation and their response doesn't hold more or less value just because they can or can't express empathy in a way that someone wants.

An example of hypo-empathy might be when someone is highly stimulated and therefore more sensitive and overwhelmed. Their expression of empathy might be reduced or dulled as they are so overwhelmed by their internal workings that reacting to external things might not be possible. This can happen during burnout or depressive episodes; someone is so low on additional capacity that they are less able to respond in a way that might be coded as empathetic to another person. They simply don't have the mental and physical resources to provide empathy.

An example of hyper-empathy could be feeling and reflecting the emotions of people around you; it can feel almost as if your emotions fill the air and take up physical space. Instead of being unable to relate to the thoughts and emotions of people around you, someone who is hyper-empathetic might instead experience people's thoughts and emotions as if they are palpable and tangible things. This can be incredibly draining. While others might be able to disengage from another's feelings that are expressed through their verbal and non-verbal communication, a person who is hyper-empathic might not find this to be possible. For me, if I see a child hurt themselves and start to cry, I am more than likely also going to end up crying because it hurts me to see them hurt. I often must push that response back to be the adult in the room and help them feel better, get a plaster, or just have a chill-out moment.

So, it's not true that we lack empathy. We can sometimes just have too much empathy and not know what to do with it all.

## Myths about what autistic people can and can't do
## Myth: autistic people can't have relationships or live independently

What an absolute outright lie! Autistic people have friends and romantic partners and can choose to live independently. The point is we have the choice. We may or may not choose to do these things, but no one else has the right to tell us that we can't, apart from the other person in the relationship. This myth comes from the negative view that society has of those with a disability and specifically of learning disabilities. Those with a learning disability are painted as unable to live with any independence and with no interest in a relationship with others – romantic or otherwise.

The scrap of truth in this myth is that we might find some of these things harder than a non-autistic person, but that doesn't mean we don't want to have meaningful relationships, share a life with someone else, or get married. For some people, these things might not be the right path for them, but to assume that all autistic people can't have a relationship is a harmful generalization. Often finding the person that you want to spend time with, have things in common with, and who treats you how you want and deserve to be treated is not an easy journey. It might take a short or long time to find the person that fits with you, as it can do for anyone.

Autistic people are often simultaneously desexualized by society and hypersexualized. Our romantic and sexual autonomy is taken away from us because we are disabled and 'disabled people can't be in relationships'. In the same breath, we are often hypersexualized through our differences with tropes like the 'manic pixie dream girl', who is aloof, blunt, and quirky (all things that have been associated with autism). What I'd love is for people to give autistic people space to take charge of their own sexuality and romantic wants.

As much as anyone else, autistic people can live independently if enabled through the right support to do so. Some things might make living independently a little bit harder.

These things mean that there are more struggles to figure out how to live independently in a way that works for you, but this doesn't diminish your ability to live independently. Importantly, independence does not have to mean living alone and doing everything alone. Independent living could be living with friends, romantic partners, or family members. It could mean cooking meals or looking after a home (by yourself or with the support of others), learning, working, or volunteering in the areas that you want to. Independence does not mean doing things without support, it means doing the things that you choose to do, having that choice and utilizing it. No one should ever take your choices away from you.

The idea that we, as autistic people, can't be in a romantic relationship or live independently is a myth. These things can be done in a variety of ways that may not fit the conventional image society has of these situations.

### Myth: autistic people can't have a job

Autistic people might have lower employment rates than other disabled people. Statistics from the UK's Office for National Statistics (February 2022) indicate that only 29.0 per cent of autistic adults are in any form of employment.[6] While this is shocking and disheartening to see, it highlights an opportunity for change. For many autistic people, employment is not accessible or welcoming, and their needs are not supported in the workplace. Employment can be made accessible for those who want to access it and workplaces can be welcoming environments that enable people to pursue careers that they find fulfilling if they choose to.

To create this change there are a lot of things that need to happen because there are a lot of steps to employment. So

6   Sparkes, I., Riley, E., Cook, B., & Machuel, P. (2022). Outcomes for disabled people in the UK: 2021. Office for National Statistics. Retrieved 29 June 2022, from https://www.ons.gov.uk/peoplepopulationandcommunity/healthandsocialcare/disability/articles/outcomesfordisabledpeopleintheuk/2021

many things go into finding, applying for, getting, and keeping a job, and there are so many different types of jobs in different areas, with different tasks and different levels of work and responsibility.

I do think also, though, that there is a radical need to value people not solely for what they offer or provide to society through their productivity, but just as people. People should be able to pursue the things they enjoy and worth shouldn't be attached to the things they enjoy or spend their time doing. Volunteering or just enjoying something should not be valued less than working at something full time.

For some people, full-time employment might be the right thing, especially when adapted to their needs and in an area they enjoy that makes use of their skills. For some, working part time, volunteering, or working more flexibly is much more suited to their inclusion or access needs, any co-occurring conditions, or just how they want to balance their life.

There are many hurdles in our current systems of employment practice that aren't explicitly exclusionary but still manage to make it difficult but not impossible for autistic people to find employment. Employment is an option open to all autistic people and is not something that is a measure of your worth as a person. Unfortunately, in a capitalist culture promoting the idea that we need to be a productive member of society, it can feel difficult when you don't fit the ideal of producing, earning, and doing.

## Myths about what autism is
### Myth: autism is a learning disability
Autism isn't a learning disability, but autistic people can have a learning disability alongside being autistic. Often the media has presented autistic people through two lenses: the first being the savant stereotype in which the person is very intelligent and has poor social skills; the second is someone who

is autistic and has a learning disability that is demonstrated through their behaviour, speech, or movement.

Someone with a learning disability has a reduced cognitive ability when compared with people without a learning disability. This cognitive difference may result in difficulty with everyday activities or taking longer to develop new skills. Learning disabilities are lifelong and can be mild, moderate, severe, or profound and multiple depending on how much their learning disability impacts their day-to-day life. With the right support, people with learning disabilities can lead independent lives, making the choices that they want and living the life they choose to live.

Ultimately, learning disability is a term, diagnosis, or category that is used to describe a range of brain or thinking differences that may impact how someone communicates, understands new or complex information, or learns new skills. Described like this, a learning disability and autism might seem very similar; however, autism typically includes social differences that a learning disability does not, and a learning disability includes differences in someone's cognition or learning. Neither autism nor a learning disability is a limit on what a person can achieve or what they can do – they just might do it differently.

Someone with a learning disability or an autistic person may need help with the management of their everyday tasks or with living independently. Although they're not the same condition, autism and learning disabilities share some of the same access needs and ways to include us, but can also differ greatly.

## Myth: autism is a mental health disorder

In the UK autism has been categorized as a mental health condition according to the Mental Health Act (1983), but this has been changed in recent planned updates to the Mental Health Act announced in 2021. Previously, autistic people could be detained under the Mental Health Act simply for being autistic (although they shouldn't have been), but now we can only be detained under the Mental Health Act if we have a mental health condition or 'mental disorder' as the Act defines it.

Autism has also been seen as a mental health condition because the origins of autism are rooted in psychiatry. As we've been defined through psychiatry, psychopathology, and atypical developmental psychology using the DSM and the ICD, a lot of the understanding about autism has always been about autism as a mental health condition or deviation from the 'norm'. The system is currently set up to understand autism through a mental health lens because even from the start we are diagnosed within mental health services. Mental health is intrinsically linked with understanding autism.

It is more useful to think of how autism is defined by autistic people and the shifts that we're starting to see within psychiatry itself. These shifts include the updated DSM-5, which although it classifies autism as a mental disorder, has moved autism into a subcategory – neurodevelopmental disorder. When we understand autism as a neurodevelopmental disorder or – my preferred wording – as a neurodevelopmental condition, it shifts us away from the incorrect idea of autism being a mental health condition.

Autism is clearly not a mental health condition, but there are many mental health conditions that autistic people can have. Autism shapes our experiences of mental health conditions and how we respond to treatments but shouldn't be seen as a mental health condition in itself. Many mental health conditions are treatable or curable, and autism is neither of these things.

## Stereotype: there is a specific autism look – 'you don't look autistic' or 'we're all a little bit autistic'

I almost but don't quite wish there was a bit of truth in there being an 'autism look'; it would make it easier to find other autistic people. Whenever someone tells me I don't look autistic, what they really mean is I don't fit with the view they hold in their head of what I should be doing, or how I should be reacting, or that I'm not what they've been told autism is. This one is just such a ludicrous statement that I probably treat it too flippantly when I hear it, questioning people on what they think autism should look like or how I should behave to match their expectations.

Another one of the phrases you're bound to hear as an autistic person is 'we're all a little bit autistic, aren't we?', except we're not. We're either autistic or we aren't, as we gathered with the pregnancy analogy earlier on. We're autistic before we know we are or someone else tells us, and people who aren't autistic just plainly aren't autistic. People might have autistic traits, aspects of autism that they also experience, but this doesn't make them a little bit autistic. Instead, it means they might be a bit sensitive to noise, they might not enjoy social situations, or they don't like wearing scratchy clothing.

My go-to responses on what autism is or looks like generally revolve around these key elements:

1. No one can be a little bit autistic; it doesn't work like that. Someone is autistic or they aren't and what you see is someone's autistic expression through their behaviours and actions. This means you can't judge someone as very autistic or a little bit autistic by looking at them.
2. What do you expect autism to look like and why don't you think I look autistic to you (this is if I'm feeling particularly confrontational and normally makes someone scramble for a response so as not to be seen as rude)?
3. People might experience autistic traits, but these aren't the same as the autistic experience of the world. Being annoyed by loud noises is not the same as loud noises being physically painful, which they are for me.
4. Autism looks different for everybody. I don't act like an autistic child because I'm now an autistic adult who has learnt to mask and manage when I find things difficult.

## Myths and causes of autism
### Myth: autism is caused by vaccines

This myth comes from a now infamous and retracted research paper by Andrew Wakefield that was published in the *Lancet* in 1998[7] at the height of misunderstanding about the measles, mumps, and rubella (MMR) vaccine. More people were getting diagnosed with autism, and the understanding of autism became much better as we moved into the twenty-first century. Parents became frightened as they saw vaccines as having a causal link to a condition that they saw as negative, but vaccines don't cause autism. What any good researcher will shout is that correlation (more people getting an autism diagnosis and more people getting an MMR vaccine) does not equal causation. Just because the two events coincided doesn't mean one caused the other.

The confusion or misattribution relates to when the MMR vaccine is given and a whole industry of misinformation that has been able to thrive. The MMR vaccine is given in two doses, one at about a year old and the booster jab at three years and four months old for those in the UK (other vaccine schedules might differ slightly). Parents began to worry as the age at which the MMR jabs are given is normally when autistic behaviours start to show; ironically these behaviours would have been there all along, but parents began to link them to the vaccine.

However, research has overwhelmingly shown that vaccines have absolutely no link to autism. Researchers in Australia compiled research on over one million children and

---

7   Wakefield, A. J., Murch, S. H., Anthony, A., Linnell, J., Casson, D. M., Malik, M., ... & Walker-Smith, J. A. (1998). RETRACTED: Ileal-lymphoid-nodular hyperplasia, non-specific colitis, and pervasive developmental disorder in children. https://doi.org/10.1016/S0140-6736(97)11096-0

found that neither the vaccines nor their ingredients have anything to do with autism.[8]

Put simply, vaccines and autism: no relationship.

## Myth: autism is caused by bad parenting/naughty children

To understand where this one comes from, we must delve back a bit into how understanding of autism developed and the historical context around it. Autism as a term was first coined in 1911 by German psychiatrist Eugen Bleuler to describe a part of schizophrenia. Soviet child psychiatrist Grunya Sukhareva developed this concept in 1924 and 1925. Due to 'Soviet isolationism', the West did not learn of Sukhareva's work until the twenty-first century. Leo Kanner, a Ukrainian-American psychiatrist, published his findings about autism in 1943, and Hans Asperger, an Austrian paediatrician, published his findings about autism in 1944. Asperger and Kanner are credited with shaping much of the early understanding of autism, although not all of this was a positive understanding of autism.

If you do choose to read more about Hans Asperger, I urge you to do so with caution as he was a proponent of eugenics, 'race hygiene', and Nazi views. Herwig Czech evaluated the historical evidence and compiled archival evidence of Asperger's Nazi history; the paper is accessible to all but is not an easy read.[9]

This myth relates to the historical understanding of autism, namely that autism was caused by 'refrigerator mothers'. Refrigerator mothers is a term that was associated with autism in the 1940s by Leo Kanner. The concept was built from the psychological ideas of the time, which were heavily influenced

---

8    Taylor, L. E., Swerdfeger, A. L., & Eslick, G. D. (2014). Vaccines are not associated with autism: an evidence-based meta-analysis of case-control and cohort studies. *Vaccine*, 32(29), 3623–3629. https://doi.org/10.1016/j.vaccine.2014.04.085

9    Czech, H. (2018). Hans Asperger, national socialism, and 'race hygiene' in Nazi-era Vienna. *Molecular Autism*, 9(1), 1–43. https://doi.org/10.1186/s13229-018-0208-6

by the work of Sigmund Freud, an Austrian neurologist. Freud developed the theory of psychoanalysis, which has impacted much of modern psychiatry. His work described psychological issues as stemming from childhood trauma (this is possibly a bit of an oversimplification). In the case of autism and refrigerator mothers, Kanner used this theory and term to describe mothers whose parenting style was cold and uncaring. This parenting style was then said to traumatize a child so much so that they retreated into themselves and became autistic.

To unpack this, we need to understand a few things.[10] First, what the concept of autism was at the time; second, how autism develops; and finally, the impact of parenting on autism.

The word autism comes from the Greek word for self (auto), and in its earliest understanding autism referred to people who were only interested in their own complex, internal world, nothing else. This relates to an internalized or self-focused conceptualization of autism, which to an outsider may look like a lack of interest in others, which is how Kanner conceptualized autism.

Autism is often recognized by others through an autistic person's behaviour, normally when a child gets to the age at which they begin to participate in social behaviours with others – for some from about 12 or 18 months old and often later into childhood depending on how children socialize. So, autism is seen as a visible difference to how other children interact and act. As these complex social behaviours can't be seen in infants and very young children, people began to think that autism is not present from birth, but that it develops at some point in early childhood.

This idea – that autism is something that can be caused by parents rather than being something that someone is born with – created a fear in parents. This fear stems from parents

---

10  Sorry that there is so much 'mental unpacking' in this myth – sometimes the history of autism and how things come to be is heavily layered and interconnected.

being the main source of consistent input that a child has in their early life and the early association with autism being a bad thing. Most parents don't want to be the cause of bad things happening to their child. Parenting can impact autistic people but not in a way that triggers them to develop autism; the impact of parenting is the same as it is for any child–parent relationship. Good parenting can be a protective factor, make children feel safe, and encourage curious learning, while very bad parenting can be a one-stop shop for a traumatic upbringing.

So, autism isn't caused by parenting, it's present whether a parent is or not. Neither is autism a consequence of being a naughty child, it's there our whole life so it can't be due to naughtiness. This idea plays into a stigma-laden view of autism because others see our meltdowns as tantrums and our reaction to an overwhelming world as being difficult. It fuels the stigma that parents, siblings, and autistic people experience about autism – this idea of autistic behaviour being bad behaviour that family members should stop or reduce. We aren't intentionally difficult, we're just in a world that is difficult for us to be in!

# Strengths, Differences, and Challenges

Autistic people can often be challenged by the environment we are in: it can be difficult for our sensory processing, require high amounts of socializing, or it may not accommodate our needs. While we can face difficulties due to the barriers that society puts in place for us, many of our differences from non-autistic people can be strengths.

Being autistic is not a bad thing and does not make you less than other people (you might be sick of me saying this by now); autistic people have a lot of strengths that balance out the challenges and difficulties we may face. Some of these strengths may include having exceptional attention to detail, having an increased interest in a topic that brings us joy, and the ability to offer different perspectives on questions or problems.

## How do we show our differences?

There are a few ways in which autistic people show the differences we have from non-autistic people. These differences are things like stimming, meltdowns, shutdowns, talking about our special interests, and the way we use routines to shape our lives. These autistic modes of self-expression are all things that other people might do a little bit but not to the same extent that autistic people do.

People have told me that when I get excited, I do a little shoulder shimmy; the excitement positively radiates through my body in the way that I move, starting from deep inside until the joy erupts from my shoulders. An autistic person might clap or may rock their body, run their fingers over a patterned surface, feel the textures of their skin, repeat noises and sounds to themselves, or move in a rhythmic way. There doesn't have to be a reason for our behaviour – no deeper intent – it is the natural way we show on the outside the feelings we can no longer contain inside.

Some of our autistic differences are treated as wrong, bad, childish, silly, attention-seeking, out of place, socially awkward, or weird. You are *not* wrong; these differences are never bad. You might have people who tell you to lessen these things that you do but you shouldn't; you don't have to change how you want to express yourself.

## Stimming

Stimming (self-stimulatory behaviour) is something that an autistic person does when happy or excited or sad or overwhelmed or anything in between. A non-autistic person might tap their foot, tap a pen on a table, or doodle as they do something, but it's normally just a way of fidgeting and doesn't have the same implications as stimming. There is no right or wrong time to stim. As autistic people, we act in ways that are similar but not the same as each other; our movements and ways of being are all different twists of the same kaleidoscope. We might view things through the same autistic lens, but what we see is not guaranteed to be the same.

I like to think of stimming as seeking out a specific feeling or response. I might use a tangle toy to move my hands and seek out the patterns I can make with it, or touch a specific fabric because I like the way it feels, or tug on my cheek (my skin is quite naturally stretchy). Stimming to me is just a way to move your body or verbally express yourself, to ground yourself in what you are feeling, and to release some of the energy that has built up inside.

Stimming is not limited to one way of doing something, it

really can be anything from a repeating movement, repeating words, hand movements, to making noises. Some stims are barely noticeable and some are very visible. Stimming behaviours are a way of self-regulating and shouldn't be stopped or reduced as they are an autistic person's way of managing a situation. For me, my stims can either be obvious and overt or subtle and covert. It could be chewing gum to deal with anxiety or showing my excitement or grounding myself.

## Meltdowns

A meltdown is a reaction to an overwhelming situation, a change of plans, and unexpected differences to what you expected, or simply anything that triggers the feeling of something not being right. For me meltdowns have always been like a train going off its tracks: I'm generally able to see them coming but once the train is in motion, I'm unable to stop it from derailing or crashing. I'll feel bad until the meltdown happens because the internal pressure of a meltdown feels like a physical weight on every part of my body and mind. That doesn't mean I feel completely better after having a meltdown, but it does mean that letting a meltdown run its course does somehow feel better in the long run. Meltdowns are exhausting, but feeling the crushing weight of the impending meltdown that never happens is worse than going through the physical and emotional ordeal of a meltdown. Better out than in, maybe.

Knowing about changes well in advance, low sensory environments, and knowing what to expect are all helpful for autistic people to avoid these situations. While we can't completely prevent meltdowns from happening, things can be done to mean situations don't build up to a meltdown. These smaller adaptations can mean that meltdowns are much less likely to happen because meltdowns are mainly reactions to the world being too much to deal with. When we're able to deal with everything we don't have meltdowns, but that only happens when we're supported.

When an autistic person is having a meltdown, we often have increased levels of anxiety and distress. This is often interpreted as frustration, a 'tantrum', or can look like an aggressive panic attack. It's important to understand that a meltdown is not a tantrum but is a reaction to a highly distressing situation or environment. In my case, I've often been found rocking, squeezing my nails into my hands, crying, or trying to escape. My meltdowns aren't a tantrum, they're me desperately trying to ground myself when the ground has been ripped out from underneath me.

While in a meltdown the person might injure themselves or others because of the extreme state of anxiety their body is in. This isn't usually intentional, it's a primal expression of self. To try and avoid a meltdown, the best thing is to use pre-emptive planning that mitigates triggers; for example, reducing anxiety related to uncertainty by providing information and agendas, details of activities, and timings before events and sticking to them. Preventing meltdowns from occurring is unfortunately the best support for a meltdown.

Other ways to reduce the likelihood of a meltdown are ensuring that we spend time in enabling environments that don't overwhelm our senses and that our access needs are met. If you can't be in an environment that works for you, having an exit strategy also works for me; a knowing look at someone who can help you make a swift exit really helps. Sometimes the impoliteness of not saying goodbye is far outweighed by the benefits of leaving somewhere before you become overwhelmed.

Meltdowns are exhausting. They are a natural way of releasing energy when overwhelmed, but that takes an awful lot of energy to do. Whenever I've had a meltdown, I've always felt completely out of control of my body, pushed over the edge by a series of small internal battles until finally the last thing, no matter how big or how small, tips me over the edge.

When I'm on the verge of a meltdown, I can physically feel it building and getting ready to unleash. Once the process of building up to a meltdown starts it can't be stopped; it simply must happen. You might learn your triggers and what this pre-meltdown feeling is for you. In meltdown situations, all you can do is prepare and hope that when the meltdown does occur you are in a safe place with someone to help you through it.

## Shutdowns

Shutdowns are often the result of situations with high demand in one or several of the following areas: social situations, situations that require a lot of thinking, lack of sleep, very emotional situations, and those that are very active or physical. Shutdowns are different to meltdowns. While a meltdown can feel like an explosion of overwhelm that's externally visible, a shutdown is much more internal and can feel like you're unable to respond to the overwhelming situation. I generally lose all verbal communication skills, my eyes widen, and I look scared or skittish.

An analogy for shutdowns that I've used to explain them to non-autistic people is that shutdowns are a bit like a computer trying to turn on, but it can't because there isn't enough power to do so. In a shutdown, we might not seem like ourselves because we're so overwhelmed that our focus must shift to only the basic functions. As we have a reduced ability to process what is going on because there is just so much going on, we may struggle to communicate as we normally would. This can mean that we become mute or have a lot of difficulty forming coherent sentences.

The best and only remedy for a shutdown is leaving the overwhelming space or activity, going somewhere less overwhelming to rest and recover, and generally just being left alone. When experiencing a shutdown, we can't have any more demands placed upon us, we just need to be given space. Shutdowns are normally a response to stress, so reducing stress is the best way to start to feel better. Unfortunately, figuring out what is stressful in a moment in which you are stressed or distressed isn't that easy; that detective work is best left until later. Depending on how you feel after a shutdown, a debrief with someone might be useful to help learn from what happened in case it happens again.[1]

## Special interests

Many autistic people have very keen interests; these interests are much stronger interests than non-autistic hobbies (we can have hobbies too). They often bring a lot of joy and can be used to soothe during times of discontent or distress and to develop an interest in new tasks or activities. These interests are often called special interests, which can feel a little bit patronizing as a term, but I don't know an alternative that is any better or explains just how important these interests are to us. Autistic people may have one special interest or many and they might last for a short but intense amount of time or an extended length of time – months, years, or even decades.

Special interests can be in any topic, category, activity, or object. Anything really. My special interests have fluctuated amongst all books, Harry Potter, Florence and the Machine, cross stitch, the London Underground, and my university. Currently, my special interest is, of all things, the M40 (a motorway that connects London and Birmingham while navigating through the Chiltern Hills with some of the best service stations in England). I could go on and write the rest of the book about the M40 but it's probably best not to as it doesn't necessarily help people to build a positive autistic identity.

An autistic special interest is broadly defined as something that an autistic person thinks about often and knows a lot about (more than your average person knows about their

---

1   I've written about burnout in the 'Autism and Physical (Ill) Health' chapter, but it is also something that is closely linked to meltdowns and shutdowns for many people. You might find it useful to read about burnout alongside meltdowns, shutdowns, and camouflaging/masking. For some people, increased meltdowns and shutdowns can be a sign of the onset of or just being in the middle of a period of burnout.

interests). A special interest might be so intense, in a good way, that you want to spend lots of your time thinking about and doing things related to it. This might be spending time thinking about or doing things related to your special interest at home, visiting places related to your special interest, or researching more about your special interest.

A special interest might be broad or general in its focus on a topic, for example, science, gardening, crafts, cars, countries, or music. Or it may be specific or niche, for example, succulents, watercolour painting, Ford cars, the flags of countries, or a specific band. Our interest in our chosen subjects might be fleeting, the intensity fuelling the interest for a week, or it may last longer and provide the passion behind a career. It's alright to change and develop new special interests, and for them to evolve with you as you evolve and change. It's also completely okay to hold these things close and not to change them; you never have to grow out of something that brings you joy. However, if you are hurt by your special interest or the pursuit of it, then it might not be the best or safest thing for you to spend time doing.

You might have come across the stereotype that all autistic people are interested in trains, collecting objects, or building Lego. These stereotypes do have a little bit of truth to them: trains are very cool and things like the London Underground have so many facts about them that can be categorized, collected, and explored in an almost therapeutic way. Collecting and categorizing objects can be incredibly relaxing and something to have pride in. If someone collects stamps or objects that have a special meaning to them, then that's really cool.

While some people might have special interests that last a long time or go through different special interests throughout their life, it's also completely normal for an autistic person not to have a special interest. You might have many special interests at once, you might just have one, or you might have none. The number of special interests that you are juggling might change as new interests enter and leave your life.

Ultimately, special interests are a special and precious thing that is unique to autistic people. While others might just think of them as hobbies we're obsessed with or something we spend too much time thinking about, special interests are just that – special. They are often something that brings unique joy and reassurance, which you can't say for every hobby or interest. Whether you have one, some, or many special interests, just know that they are an important part of your life and there will always be someone who will want to hear you info-dump about your special interest. Sometimes you might need to look a bit harder than you'd like to find a person who will listen.

Not all special interests last forever; sometimes they're with you through a tough time and lose some of their importance as you move on to a new interest. They could last days, weeks, months, years, or a lifetime. The duration isn't something that decides how important they are to you. When a special interest fades you might feel sadness, emptiness, or grief for what was once incredibly meaningful for you. Sometimes it might fade gently and others it might leave with a bang of emotion. It's okay to feel and process that change in a way that suits you, big or small, at the time or later on.

## Routines, certainty, and safety

Most of us use routines to some extent to shape our days from going to school, to working, to how we get ready for things and the ways we unwind from tension. Routines can be as complex as every action you take to get ready in the morning or as familiar as the route from A to B; that is, if you're like me and don't deviate from a chosen route between two destinations once you've found the perfect route. I mean, why mess with perfection when you know it exists?

Autistic people are often described as preferring repetition or sameness, whether that be in our daily routines or behaviours like stimming. Repetitive things like routines or stimming are often incredibly reassuring: they can be predicted, they're the same, and they're safe. They're reliable when many other things aren't.

Routines might be used to soothe anxiety by creating structure in activities. This might be especially important in things like self-care and hygiene, what to do to get ready for the day, what to do before having or preparing food, what to do while washing, or what to do before going to bed. Simplifying these routines to make them as reassuring as possible or reducing routines to as few steps as possible is something that many autistic people do to manage the demands that might be placed upon them.

If we take the example of getting ready in the morning, there are many points where this all might seem too much.

1. Setting an alarm and getting up with enough time to do everything you need to do to leave the house on time. How long is enough time? If you're like me, how do you build in time to be anxious and worry about the rest of the day? For other people that might just be contingency time for other things taking longer than the amount of time you think they will take.

2. Getting out of bed, using the toilet, brushing your teeth, showering, brushing your hair, and any skincare you might do. I've grouped all of these into one step as they all relate to hygiene, but there are many steps involved, some of which autistic people might struggle with. Brushing your teeth is difficult for some autistic people due to the potential for sensory hell from the tactile and auditory overwhelm of toothbrushes, and the taste and smell of the toothpaste. Washing yourself takes a lot of energy. Some people might be sensory seeking and enjoy water, while others might be aversive, and this might not fit with how often different parts of your body need washing. For some people washing their hair every day is not healthy for their hair, but they may

wash their body once a day or twice if they exercise heavily. As someone with energy-limiting conditions alongside being autistic, I find hygiene exhausting, but some others find showers to be very refreshing.

3. Choosing clothes and getting dressed. This can be a difficult one. You've got to contend with the weather, the occasion, and the activity that you're undertaking. Some people thrive on choosing what to wear, some rely on favourite fabrics or outfits, and others might wear the same thing to save on decision-making.

4. Deciding on, making, and eating breakfast. Food can be tricky and deciding on a sensorily fulfilling breakfast that is time appropriate to make, enjoyable, and fills you up until lunchtime can be a lot to juggle. For some people food is a struggle if they have a difficult relationship with food; for others, planning is a struggle as there are so many options for breakfast.

5. Planning your agenda for the day and what activities you will do and when. This is something people might do the day or week beforehand depending on how far in advance you plan the things you want to do.

6. Getting your things ready for the day and preparing to leave home for the day if your planned activities are outside (like school or work). Making sure you have everything packed that you might need for the day can take a bit of planning and figuring out.

Quite a lot goes into a morning routine! For some people, the separate routines that go into a 'simple morning routine' can be straightforward to put together, but juggling all these routines, actions, and needs might not always be easy for autistic people. Some people manage this through 'now and next' planning, visual reminders, or through a long process of developing routines into sustained habits that drain less mental planning energy and feel much more instinctual or memorized.

The certainty of routines is helpful for autistic people to provide reassurance about situations or experiences that provoke anxiety. Anxiety occurs where uncertainty lies, so providing certainty and security is a way of alleviating potential or actual anxiety. Routines give that security; finding out what is happening and building a mental scaffold or social script of a situation also creates that sense of concreteness, clarity, and certainty about a situation.

To further build certainty or clarity into interactions, we might use social scripting techniques such as pre-planning conversations or phrases, practising facial expressions or body language, knowing who we will interact with and the kinds of things they like to talk about, or planning how long to socialize for.

## Non-verbal communication

We all use a whole range of non-verbal communication methods to add extra understanding to what we say aloud, but not everyone understands or picks up on these non-verbal communication methods. These ways of 'saying *without* saying' include eye contact, body language, facial expressions, tone of voice, and where we physically position ourselves when spending time with other people. Demystifying and figuring out what people are 'saying' with their non-verbal communication is something that a lot of autistic people struggle with when compared with non-autistic people.

Non-verbal communication is meant to be a thing you can decode reflexively or automatically – something that is meant to come naturally to people – but that's not true for autism. It's very much not a reflex we have; instead of being easy it's incredibly energy-consuming to have to manually flip a processing switch that is so automatic for others.

We must learn as best as we can to decode the meaning that others are implying without their words. This is made more difficult by not always receiving the signals to interpret in the first place if we don't always make eye contact or if we can't figure out someone's tone of voice in the auditory scramble conversations tend to take place in.

So as not to annoy everyone around me, I've spent my entire life building a mental encyclopaedia of different head movements, body language, intonations, hand gestures, pacing movements, and everything else under the umbrella of non-verbal communication. I still might not know exactly what everything means or get my interpretation right 100 per cent of the time, but I do have some successes in figuring out what others are communicating – it just takes a huge amount of energy that others don't see being spent. This means socializing can often lead to huge amounts of fatigue or a social hangover that needs to be recovered from.

However, it is not all doom, gloom, and just us trying to fit in, communication problems can go both ways. Autistic people can have forms of different non-verbal communication to non-autistic people. We might cross our arms because we need to feel pressure, or we might tap our feet because we are stimming. This can confuse non-autistic people (who might interpret arm-crossing as hostile and foot-tapping as impatience), but we might be understood by other autistic people.

Non-verbal communication isn't just about what you do. It's also about what other people think. People can guess how someone feels from their non-verbal communication but may make mistakes. Non-verbal communication has a lot of parts to it. You are using your voice, face, and body to communicate with someone. That person is also responding to you with their voice, face, and body. You also need to figure out what they are trying to say with what they are communicating. All of this happens at the same time, in split seconds of processing or understanding, and it can be hard to deal with it all at once.

Autistic people might try to communicate with just our words instead. We make sure people can understand what we say, and that we understand what other people say. This works if the people we talk to can also just focus on words, but non-autistic people have a hard time doing that. They search for additional meaning in everything else we aren't saying.

## Eye contact (or the lack of it)

Non-autistic people seem obsessed with eye contact: whether we give eye contact, whether we avoid it, whether we only sometimes look at someone, if we're paying attention to them or not, and they always seem to want to know what we're looking at and why. A lot of autistic people don't make eye contact; some might only make eye contact some of the time or only with some people. Some can't focus on the words that others say when making eye contact as it is too much to process at once, and for some, it is physically painful. This is something that some non-autistic people just don't understand about eye contact: we're not being rude. Not looking someone in the eyes is not us lying to them, it is us enabling ourselves to process what they're saying or not putting ourselves through pain. Eye contact is overrated – in no way does it make sense that you have to look at someone's eyes to listen to what they say.

I've always been a bit in the middle: I'm generally able to look at someone while they're talking, but it isn't always their eyes I'm looking at – it's the furrow of their brow, their hand movements, or the way their mouth forms the words they're saying. Some of these ironically are taken as flirting tactics; they're absolutely not flirtatious behaviours for me, they're processing behaviours! I just find it difficult to make eye contact. It's not about pain or processing, my brain just 'nopes' out of the situation. For me eye contact isn't good or bad, it's neutral and, for some reason, my brain doesn't want to compute it. I'm not being intentionally aloof or avoiding people, it's just how I am.

Eye contact is used by non-autistic people to try to figure out people's emotions or feelings. This is where we get phrases like 'a smile that reaches someone's eyes' or 'sad eyes' or 'fiery eyes filled with anger' or 'world-weary eyes'. Non-autistic people treat eyes as 'the window to the soul', a phrase it is hard for me to understand until I put an overly analytical hat on. To them, eyes provide a huge amount of emotional meaning that they are built to understand; we are not built that way, we can learn through extensive trial and error our whole lives. Understanding eye contact is a two-way thing: people read others' emotions through eye contact and express their emotions through their own eyes. That might be why non-autistic eye contact-makers love it: they use it to figure out what everyone else is thinking and say the same thing but without words.

This is where we differ from non-autistic people. They rely on subtext and reading between the lines, figuring things out from their interpretations of what someone isn't saying. We are more explicit; we will say how we're feeling or what we're thinking instead of laying breadcrumbs for (mis)interpretation. You don't need eye contact for what someone says plainly.

Eye contact isn't something all autistic people can't do or don't want to do. Some autistic people do share eye contact with others. They might learn how to do it in a way that isn't painful or doesn't impact their processing ability. For some, this might be looking at someone's nose, eyebrows, or the space in between. This is technically pretending to give eye contact but meets the wants of non-autistic people for us to look deeply into their eyes (or near enough their eyes). Others might look another person in the eyes and not feel discomfort or awkward doing so; we're all different and that might be their norm.

### Unspoken social rules that make zero sense

We're meant to understand social rules and abide by them; we're told that these rules don't change and that they make sense. They don't. We're told to be honest but not completely honest and to lie during times when others would benefit from the lie but not to lie when the truth might be more appropriate. However, we must judge the appropriateness by ourselves, and we can't get it wrong. Simple, right?

Social rules are not strict rules as such – they're guidelines that people follow because other people have told them to. There are some rules we're expected to adhere to in social situations as they arise:

*We say hello* to someone as they enter a space and make them feel welcomed. This is generally regardless of whether you like someone or not, and whether you talk to them often or not. This is considered polite by those around you and is considered a 'social lubricant' – acting in a way that makes things easier for other people.

*Asking people how they are*, what they've been up to, whether they have any news, and remembering to ask about updates they've given in the past is something that is expected of us. We're meant to carry with us a mental encyclopaedia of how everyone's lives are progressing and how they entangle with everyone else's. Again, this means the polite and socially acceptable thing to do is to rifle through our internal records about everyone and ask about the details of their lives to provide them a space to update us on what they're doing.

*Interrupting people is rude*, but people do it all the time. People talk over others, and sometimes it's okay and other times it isn't. There is a secret hierarchy to be decoded as to who is 'allowed' to interrupt or speak over others, and you're also not really allowed to point that out in case it offends someone. I generally try not to interrupt people but there are some instances in which it is allowed, for example, if you have an emergency, when there is a lull in the conversation, or when it seems like someone has completed their point.[2] I've found that this no interruptions rule is mainly to stop autistic people info-dumping or barging into a conversation with our points.

---

2   This can get complex, however, as sometimes it feels or seems like someone has finished their point, but the cues we look out for in language and communication don't always work and people aren't always finished talking.

*We have indoor voices and outside voices.* You shouldn't raise your voice inside; you need to speak loud enough to be heard and when talking outside you can be louder but not too loud. Autistic people are said to talk too loudly and seem unaware that this isn't okay; we're unfairly judged for sharing our excitement in the volume of our voices mainly because it's deemed socially unacceptable. We apparently don't have the same internal microphone as other people so might not realize when we're talking too loudly or too quietly.

When someone asks, 'How are you?', *they aren't actually asking about how you are,* they're lining the question up for you to answer with 'I'm fine'. As autistic people we might actually want to tell the truth – that we aren't fine – and often people can't handle that. They don't want to talk about it – they want to keep things light and not dive below the surface.

*Conversation is a to and fro.* It's polite to treat conversation like a tennis volley, passing the conversation ball from person to person rather than hogging the ball and info-dumping. We're told that we should only talk briefly to let other people talk, and only to talk about the things of interest to other people or relevant to the conversation. That can be difficult when you're passionate about a topic and want to share it with people – especially during a conversation that isn't always that interesting.

*When someone is talking to you, you need to look interested:* interested in what they are saying, study their body language, understand what they are saying, and convey an emotion that matches the emotional scene they are creating. If someone is happy about something, we need to look enthusiastic, and if they are sad, we need to convey concern. Sometimes this interest needs to be faked; it's not a bad thing but a coping thing, looking like you're interested can make a social situation run more smoothly.

Thinking of them this way, these rules all seem rather fake or flimsy, don't they? They're not technically written down but are deeply ingrained and knitted into the social fabric that makes up our society; some would say they hold society together.

Importantly, also, social rules only relate to specific societies or cultures with there often being many differences between cultures as to what is socially acceptable or expected. What is the epitome of polite behaviour in one culture could be incredibly rude in another. As well as not translating culturally, social rules often don't translate autistically. We're expected to know all these rules when we just aren't built to; you can't know a rule if the very things that aren't meant to be pointed out aloud (social rules) are never spoken about out loud. We can't know what isn't said, isn't obvious, or isn't consistent. As autistic people we thrive on things being explicit rather than obscured; instead, we must figure it out for ourselves, potentially making multiple social faux pas along the way.

These rules don't come easily or simply to us. I joke about how silly social rules are, and I often find a bit of internal fun at how ridiculous some of them are as I observe them rigidly play out. However, I do find that attempting to follow them, in places and situations where it doesn't feel safe not to follow these rules, is the best way to go. Figuring out the best way to socialize is a very active process. I've said it already, but it's completely exhausting; non-autistic people might sometimes get tired after a lot of socializing but it's nowhere near the same level as autistic social fatigue. We can't always give the energy needed to follow these social rules as well as other people would want us to. Plus, following these rules often benefits them more than us, particularly if your self-esteem is high enough not to worry about how others view and think about you.

A lot of autistic people spend a lot of time trying to figure out the rules. We might come up with our own ways to understand the rules or come up with our own rules. This is a lot of work.

## Masking and camouflaging

Some autistic people can appear very able in social situations – so much so that it might be difficult to see that we are autistic. This is intentional. We observe the social movements of non-autistic people and mirror or mimic their behaviours to hide our autistic-ness. We might do this because it is the 'easiest' thing to do if we don't want to share our autistic identity or we don't want to go into the level of detail needed to explain autism. While everyone tends to socially perform in any given situation to appear their 'best self', we may mask being autistic or the behaviours deemed visibly autistic in a way that is different to non-autistic social performance.

This means that we can appear to be fine and coping or sometimes even excelling in a social situation, but often reap the repercussions and effects of performing that can become evident afterwards. A lot of energy goes into either trying to appear not autistic or as if socializing is easy. The following are some behaviours that are considered masking, camouflaging, or social compensation behaviours:

- Forcing or faking eye contact during conversations as that's what non-autistic people do and feel comfortable doing.
- Imitating or copying facial expressions to mirror another's emotional mood and body language. This can include borrowing or copying gestures that you have seen others do.
- Not talking about your special interests or feigning lack of interest in them if they aren't deemed cool enough by others (I know the M40 isn't cool so I save talking about it for safer spaces where I can happily nerd out).
- Using social scripts or fixed responses to questions that might come up in conversation. Basically, anything that involves preparing for conversations by rehearsing what responses might be needed.
- Pretending that loud spaces aren't loud and don't cause

sensory overload or that flashing lights are fun and don't cause sensory overload. You might push through the sensory overload or overwhelm to stay in a place longer because non-autistic people wouldn't be impacted by busy crowds, loud noises, or other sensory inputs.

- Not stimming as that isn't something non-autistic people do. You might instead use more covert stims that aren't as obviously autistic; other people might think you are fidgeting rather than stimming.

We might do some of these things without paying attention to them; they can be ingrained into how we act and socialize, becoming almost second nature with years of masking. It can be difficult to unmask or feel comfortable in a social situation with others while being your authentic autistic self. It's a process and one that is often filled with a lot of self-discoveries. I didn't realize how big a deal masking was for me or how much of myself I had lost to creating this mask until I could look back at it all.

After my diagnosis and after finding the autistic community online, I began to learn more about the terms masking and camouflaging as others shared their experiences. I found that although the terms were completely new to me, they described my experiences completely and utterly. I finally had language to explain my internal world. In 2017 I found a research paper[3] by Laura Hull and other camouflaging researchers. It unravelled an entirely new concept for me. They gave me language for something I'd done for so long without knowing how to describe it. The paper also sparked quite an intense special interest in trying to find out more about autistic masking and camouflaging.

---

3   Hull, L., Petrides, K. V., Allison, C., Smith, P., Baron-Cohen, S., Lai, M. C., & Mandy, W. (2017). 'Putting on my best normal': social camouflaging in adults with autism spectrum conditions. *Journal of Autism and Developmental Disorders, 47*(8), 2519–2534. https://doi.org/10.1007/s10803-017-3166-5

What I sadly hadn't realized in my investigations around masking was that I had spent my whole life masking my true self in every social interaction. I had done this so completely that my autistic self and the self I showed to the world ended up becoming utterly intertwined. So much so that I have no clue who the real me is now. I didn't have an opportunity when I was younger to positively affirm my autistic identity; instead, I had been constantly told that the autistic parts of me needed to be hidden or lessened. So, I hid them and lessened them.

That's why I think diagnosis younger, learning about yourself younger, having the terms to understand yourself younger, and forming a supportive community of autistic people around you younger are so important. If this had happened to me, I don't think I would've developed such a fluent and comprehensive mask. I would know my true self. I wouldn't have had to spend years later untangling everything to try to figure out who I am.

While it's unfair to say there aren't some bits of truth in the masks I created to navigate different social situations, masking has unfortunately also led to anxiety and a real crisis of confidence as to who I am and who I am allowed to be in certain spaces. We mask to protect ourselves, and a mask is a great source of protection in the moment, but the consequences do always follow (sometimes at a delay). Things like losing our sense of self, increased suicidal ideation, and exhaustion are scary possible outcomes to face. Instead of instantly unmasking just because we know it's bad for us, some of us might continue to mask because it does provide a bit of social ease where we might not find it otherwise.

### What does masking feel like?

As someone who is a bit of a social chameleon, able to blend into any social scene and melt into whatever a social situation demands of me, I'm often told I'm a person that wears multiple hats. People remark on how well I get along in social situations 'despite being autistic' if they know me. If they don't know me, they often say 'I never would have guessed you were autistic' if I tell them and are none the wiser if I don't. I have a certain ability to quickly decode social spaces, find the best way to communicate with whoever is there, and come across as confident, eloquent, and socially savvy. All of this is a bit of pretence, a charade, a performance, and ultimately something that takes a bunch of energy that I don't even realize I'm burning through.

My relationship with being autistic hasn't always been perfect or filled with the pride I've always wished I had. I might preach positivity about being autistic, but I've not always felt that positivity. It's a journey. I've often masked. My true, authentic autistic identity gets hidden to protect against the crushing, although not always deliberate, stigma the revelation of an autism diagnosis results in.

Ultimately, this means that in every social situation, I am constantly assessing whether I need to mask or not. I use inexplicable amounts of mental and physical energy to appear less autistic or non-autistic through mimicry and replication of non-autistic social behaviours. It's weird feeling the pressure of wanting to fit in when you know the real you might not. It's also a relief to know that there are spaces where this is not true.

So, I (we) face an ultimatum: to mask or to face the uncertainty of how someone will react when I tell them I'm autistic. I don't enjoy playing around with this uncertainty, so I make myself smaller and fold away the autistic parts of myself as the world has somehow made me think that's easier. It's easier on the world for me to take on the mental load of deciding not to concisely explain autism positively, not to challenge stigma or stereotypes, and not to share my needs. Instead, on the days that I do fight back and unmask, I defend my existence and correct the inaccuracies in how I've been defined.

So, sometimes I mask, but it's something I'm trying to do less often nowadays. There are still days on which I hide, and I squirrel away all the pieces of myself until I become a knotted mess of identity. I conceal the stims my hands wish to paint in the air as my body moves to a different tempo through space and anxiety. I feign confidence and comfort around big conversations that wade through the sludge of small talk. I hold my body in the vice of engaged postures and twist my body language to map, mirror, and reflect the faces looking back at me.

It's not a practice I recommend; it weighs heavy on the soul. When you step back to see the reflection in the mirror it's startling how little resemblance it bears to what you're used to. We all shape ourselves to the demands of a social situation, autistic or not, but the costs are not the same.

So, we end up with a sword so double-edged it's completely multifaceted, hiding our autistic self damages our mental health, and hiding our mental ill health worsens both our mental health and our capacity to build these protective walls. It's fairly isolating building yourself a protective space in which you can only be your true self on your own, but is that even your true self?

I wish I had the faith that masking wouldn't be necessary, but even while understanding it has a negative impact on me, I 'know' it is better than the vulnerability I'm not always prepared to face the world with. The tricks and costumes almost become a comfort as they become the dominant part of your seen identity; like a performer getting ready for a show, the rituals provide some certainty in a world that has a distinct lack of stability.

I don't know, I think masking is probably more complicated than mask on/mask off.

# Do I Need to Tell People I'm Autistic?

Sharing that you're autistic can be a momentous occasion for anyone, whether you've known you're autistic for a while or are sharing the news just after being diagnosed. I wish I could say that you only have to disclose your diagnosis once, but I can't. Unfortunately, as with any time you share part of your identity that might not be immediately obvious, telling people you're autistic isn't one 'coming out', but many. Telling people you're autistic is something that you become accustomed to; you find the script and timing that works for you once you've told some people. It isn't something that has to be done perfectly and doesn't just mean telling someone 'I'm autistic', it also means telling them what being autistic means for you.

It isn't something that should be daunting because being autistic isn't scary or bad. Unfortunately, however, it can be nerve-wracking to announce that you're autistic to someone, especially because you can't know what their reaction will be until they've reacted. We can't pre-empt everything and every eventuality, we can only plan for what we can control. We can't control how other people react. You're autistic before you tell someone, and you're autistic after; the only thing that is different is their perception of you. That's the bit that can worry people: how someone's perception changes means how they treat you might change.

It is something that has worried me in the past. Particularly when my diagnosis was fresher, and I didn't know what being autistic meant for me. Being given a new label for your experiences can shake things up a bit. Do you need to completely re-evaluate everything and recategorize your whole self because you now have new terms of understanding? Potentially not, but it can feel that way, especially when the follow-up question about your diagnosis can be 'What does that mean?' or 'Is that like [insert media portrayal of autistic people in comedies and dramas here]?'. Ultimately, we all need to understand ourselves to be able to describe ourselves, and that can change when autism or any other condition is thrown in.

Whether you tell people that you're autistic is completely up to you; it is your choice who you share that information with as it is your personal information that you have the option of sharing. We can't control everything in the world, so having control over something like whom we tell that we are autistic, when we tell them, and what that means for us feels very important. It feels important because it is.

Telling someone doesn't have to be a heavily orchestrated event. It can happen at any moment of your choosing and when you feel most comfortable sharing. Figuring out how to share about being autistic is not something that comes naturally, as often being vulnerable with near strangers doesn't feel natural, but it is something that people learn how to do over time. The experience does involve some trial and error, but 'error' is more of a learning opportunity than wholly negative. If someone has a negative reaction towards you sharing that you're autistic, then that says far more about them than it does about you. Often people's reactions can uncover barely hidden ableism, outdated stereotypes, and intolerance of difference, and show us a truth obscured by social niceties. Try not to worry too much because it can open up a world of support and understanding; sometimes my worry gets ahead of me.

I want to reiterate: it is never an error to share that you are autistic. It can feel that way if things don't go as planned or you start to focus on how someone might treat you differently after finding out. Anyone that shares part of their identity, whether it be that they are autistic or not, feels some discomfort about how someone might react. That isn't because they are ashamed of who they are, but instead, it is much more how society has told people to react to vulnerable news. Sharing parts of your identity is not shameful, it is often liberating and should be treated as such. In terms of autism, it is about explaining differences that might be noticed by others and asking for some support or help when things get too much.

For some, this might seem like 'pulling the A card' and using autism as a defence against all wrong, but that's a cynical and harmful way of looking at it. When someone shares that they are autistic this isn't done to garner sympathy but to encourage someone to empathize. It's ableist for someone to think that autism is something that means sympathy is the necessary reaction. Autism doesn't mean your life is worse.

Autism is a word that categorizes and encapsulates a specific experience of the world. Ideally someone understands what these experiences and needs are when a diagnosis is shared, but, unfortunately, that isn't always the case due to stereotypes and media portrayals of autism. There wouldn't be the same reaction for sharing other identities that are immediately obvious. For example, when someone turns up in a wheelchair, their need for ramps, lifts, and level access to buildings is not questioned (this isn't to say that accessibility is always there when needed) as that need is visible and well understood by society.

## Telling family

Telling your family, whether that be your immediate family or your wider family, that you're autistic is something that you *should* have control over. I say *should* here because while you should have the autonomy and authority to talk about your own lived experience, this is not something that we always have control over. It might not feel as if you have control over this if your parents are heavily involved with your diagnostic process, as they generally are for diagnoses made throughout childhood and young adulthood. If you are exploring a self-diagnosis of autism or an autistic identity before a formal diagnosis, this can make it easier to manage who is involved and who knows what. As formal diagnosis by its very nature involves someone who knew you growing up, typically a parent or carer, it can be difficult to completely remove them from the process. When you get to an age at which you are given more independence and control over the information about your life and identity, you can have more ownership over how information about you is shared.

Your parents might share the information on your behalf depending on what age you are diagnosed, but it is completely up to you as to how you define what autism means for you as you grow older. Our needs and actions as children don't match the self we grow up to become. How an overwhelmed autistic toddler or school-tired child acts may have some cross-over with a teen or an adult, but there is growth (emotionally, physically, and mentally) in all of that and therefore difference.

Parents may share that you're autistic or that you have autism, depending on how they speak about autism. They might talk about how that impacts them, but it remains up to you how much you talk about what autism means for you. Family members might position autism in relation to how your autism impacts them and the ways that they interact with your diagnosis. For parents, this might be the advocating they have to do for you, their actions to keep you safe, the things they have learnt about you being autistic, and the system that they battle to try and get you the best out of life. For siblings, this might be how they feel about having a sibling who doesn't fit in with what society deems as normal. This doesn't mean that a sibling relationship is completely negative or completely positive if one of you is autistic because no relationship is either one or the other – it's always a blend of both.

Relationships and understanding from family members of different generations can often be quite polarizing: some generations or family members might be quite set in their ways of understanding, and others might be more open to listening to new information. We generally get comfortable with the knowledge and understanding that we have, so can brush off perceived challenges to that. You might find that older relatives like grandparents, uncles, aunts, and more distant relations fall into this stereotype. I never got to test this hypothesis with my grandparents as they died before my diagnosis, but I have experienced this struggle with older family members who aren't always as amenable to changing their perspectives as I'd like.

It can be difficult trying to explain autism to a family member who doesn't seem to get it; it's often an uphill battle of bracing yourself against offensive language, cringing at the connections they make, and figuring out the safest way to represent or present yourself. I often find myself deciding whether or not the awkward language and understanding are the 'hills I want to die on' or the battles I want to pick. Confrontation is never easy. I find it is easier to correct the things that can be dealt with quickly and not to try to reverse the things that can't be smoothed over as easily. For example, I've had family members talk about autistic people in the news as if they're tragedies who won't lead happy lives because they're non-verbal; this is the type of thing I've challenged. I've challenged this by stopping the conversation, highlighting that the statement is harmful, and asking why they make that assumption.

It might be useful to have these conversations with family members about your autistic identity when you can or as you think of them because it might not be a topic that always comes to mind, and it changes as you grow older. Personally, as an adult, I don't talk about autism that much with my family, but it still permeates every interaction I have with family and everyone else. It's not that it's an elephant in the room, but rather my family and friends understand what autism means for me, and they don't need to ask questions as we've had those conversations previously.

## Telling friends and strangers

Disclosing your autistic identity is entirely up to you. Some people are open about their autism diagnosis with others, and some prefer not to tell many people. It can be a form of self-expression or self-preservation. When you are free to be yourself you may not need to verbalize that you are autistic as it shines through in your actions. For those who only disclose when they feel safe, disclosure might feel like the final unveiling of layers of self-preservation.

Although autism is an integral part of a person, sharing our identity can be anxiety provoking. It may feel unnecessary to share it with every single person you meet unless they need to know. If I'm popping into a shop to buy a few items I don't need to share my autistic identity unless it's necessary. If I'm going to hospital and will spend some time there, I will tell doctors, nurses, and clinical staff that I'm autistic and what that means in terms of helping me to access healthcare.

Just as autism is a spectrum of differences in how a person understands the world around them, how someone feels about being autistic or having autism is also a spectrum. For some autistic people, sharing that they are autistic is something they are very comfortable with. They may know what disables them, and what helps them, and they do not feel negative about their autistic identity. For others, it can be a completely different story: other people's perception of autism can mean that you don't feel comfortable with your autistic differences, you see autism as a deficit, or autism has always been viewed negatively or shamefully around you.

Disclosing that you're autistic can feel scary, offer a sense of relief, enable access to support, and indicate trust all at the same time. So, it is and should always be your decision to disclose what you want to say and when you want to say it. As much as we can try to tell ourselves otherwise, telling someone that we are autistic does change what someone thinks about us. Preparing to be in that situation can be useful for you, for example, by knowing your script and preparing answers for the inevitable questions that people ask us when we share that part of ourselves.

When talking about autism it can be far too easy to slip into the negatives or self-deprecating comparisons about autism. Sometimes saying 'I'm autistic and that means I can...' is difficult to do if you don't know what you do well and don't want to talk about what you can't do. When thinking about disclosing autism, it is beneficial to think about what you can do, what you struggle with, and the common stereotypes that exist about autism that are meaningful for you.

Tackling all of this is a big task and doesn't have to be done with every person you tell as each disclosure is unique – even if you tell a big group at once. We can break down this task into smaller tasks and remember that in the same way as we want to be treated as individuals, we must treat us sharing our autistic identity as an individual experience for those we share it with.

## Things to think about when telling someone you're autistic

Preparing to tell someone that you're autistic is something you can put a whole host of planning into. You can potentially prepare for every eventuality that you can imagine coming up. You can come up with all the phrases to explain exactly who you are and what that means. That doesn't mean it will all go to plan.

For me I've always dropped hints beforehand, to see what they think autism is before I jump in and explain I'm autistic. It can feel like laying a booby trap for people to fall into because you're trying to see if they mess up and say things that are hurtful about autistic people. Instead, I like to think of it as doing a background check just to make sure that I feel safe telling this person I'm autistic.

Unfortunately, even this doesn't guarantee that things will go perfectly. There might be misunderstandings about what you're saying. Someone might brush off your uncovering of this part of your identity as not that big a deal when to you it does feel like a big deal. It can feel like you're sharing something that means someone will subsequently assess all your words and movements. *How autistic are you being in your interactions with them? How well do you perform as an autistic person?* It can create extra hassle as the feeling of someone watching you doesn't necessarily go away.

My biggest piece of advice is to plan what you're going to do, think about who you're telling, and, if you want to, make the leap. Once you've shared that you're autistic you can't exactly take it back, you can only continue to shape someone's understanding from the point at which you've shared that piece of you.

## The ten key points of disclosing (to anyone)

There are many component parts to disclosing that can help it go as smoothly as possible, no matter who you're telling.

1.  Eliminate any chance of you being misunderstood. You are the person with the power in this situation to correct misinformation. You can reduce the chance of being misunderstood or misinformation being spread by knowing what you're talking about when you talk about autism. Preferably, don't be like me by saying things like 'Autism means my brain is broken' or 'Autism means I am a bad friend'.[1]

2.  Instead, I would suggest planning for what you might be asked, such as how autism impacts you, what support you might need, and how autism might impact the person you're disclosing to (if it does). It can help to have someone there whom you feel comfortable with

---

1   Some unfortunate phrases that I really used, and regret having used. We learn and grow, and I'd never use these again.

and who understands you and what autism means for you. They can support you if you get overwhelmed or receive a negative reaction.

3. Research autism and find non-stigmatizing explanations. The best way to prepare is to do your autism homework. Being an autistic person, you might get treated as the autism expert, and knowing about autism will mean you're better prepared to answer any questions that come up. You don't have to overdo the research, but knowing some of the basics should get you through. You can talk through what you struggle with, the differences you have, and things that help you. For example, saying 'I don't like to meet in loud spaces as I can't hear people very well' is a way of sharing an autistic difference without highlighting your identity outright. By building up understanding you create foundations for people to understand autism.

4. You get to choose your timing, so choose as well as you can! You choose when to tell someone, and that depends on a couple of factors. It could be that the length of the friendship or relationship means that now is the right time. There might be a gap in conversation topics to share that you are autistic. There might be enough time to dive into a longer discussion if needed or time to leave quickly if it doesn't go well. Are you in a good place for this discussion in yourself or is it better left for another moment? Is the person you want to tell in a good headspace to take on what might be a big chunk of information?

5. Timing is essential in making you both feel comfortable. It can be something you tell someone when you first meet them if it feels appropriate, but it often feels more appropriate to wait and share after you've built up some trust and a relationship first. If you know someone better, you might know the words they are much more likely to understand.

6. There is absolutely no need to rush into something you only hope to do once. Find a place where you feel comfortable sharing your identity with someone. You can tell someone at home, in a public place, or digitally by messaging them. It is important to construct a space and experience that you are comfortable with.

7. You get to choose who gets to know you. The person you tell might not know what autism is or might partially know what autism is. You don't have to treat autism like a secret – it's not a clandestine club. I've generally chosen to tell people and then have asked them not to tell others as I want to tell them in my own way. This is probably a hang-up from being bullied and wanting to be in control of sharing the part of me others bullied me for.

8. Disclosing is a personal decision. It can provide context for the way you act, how you communicate, and what support works best for you. It's your choice to share. The words you use can shape the context you provide about yourself, so try to think of words that fit with how you want to be thought of and described.

9. It might not be easy, but you can do it. It can be easier to do with a support person there; they don't necessarily have to do anything – just being there to support you emotionally and physically is enough. I always see disclosure as an incredibly quick way to find out what someone really thinks. As much as they are analysing me and what I'm saying and trying to figure out what the information I'm sharing means, I'm analysing them and their reaction to what I say.

10. No one can do the sharing for you; ultimately, it must be you – you're the one who has the words that describe yourself the best and the power to make yourself understood.

## Telling your employer that you're autistic

Telling employers and colleagues is different to telling friends or family; there are consequences, both positive and negative, that can come from these discussions. It can be difficult to pre-empt what might happen if you tell your employer or prospective employer that you are autistic. When you have a job already it can mean accessing support to enable you to thrive or at the very least to make the parts you struggle with easier to manage. When you are applying for a job it can mean adjustments to the application process, the interview, and their understanding of your needs.

As well as it being difficult to guess how others will react it can be difficult to figure out what that will mean for you. Will they understand what you mean when you talk about autism? Will they react positively to you sharing the news? Will they think that it limits you in ways that it doesn't? Will they be reluctant to deal with the extra 'burden' an autistic person adds to a workplace?

### The benefits of disclosing for employment

- The Equality Act (2010) means employers are legally obligated to put in place the reasonable adjustments that you need (you just need to know what those are first). I suggest using the DARE Report on Adjustments (2020)[2] to figure out what sort of adjustments you might want or need. In other countries, civil rights legislation offers some similar protections.
- You don't know what level of understanding people have until you share your diagnosis; it can only grow or get better from there as they realize what autism means for you and your support needs.

---

2   Heasman, B., Livesey, A., Walker, A., Pellicano, E., & Remington, A. (2020). DARE report on adjustments. Centre for Research in Autism and Education, Institute of Education, UCL, London, UK. Retrieved 10 October 2022, from https://dareuk.org/dare-adjustments-toolkit

- As we've already explored, masking or camouflaging that you are autistic is exhausting. If you share your diagnosis or identity, even if it's just with a few colleagues or managers, then you don't have to mask with them. You get to be authentically you.

## The risks of disclosing for employment

- Although people are legally obligated to do something, that doesn't mean that they always do what is needed. You might be misunderstood, and your reasonable adjustments might not be recognized. Unfortunately, adjustments being 'reasonable' is subjective and people may not view your basic access needs as reasonable.
- You might be worried about potential prejudice or discrimination from your employer or fellow employees. These might not be big displays of discrimination and can often be micro-aggressions that wear you down.

To help you decide whether to disclose and when, try drawing up a list of pros and cons for disclosing. This could be what you want to say, how you want to say it, who you want to start with, and when you want to disclose. You could try asking a friend for help with this, a colleague you get along with well, or an advisor; sometimes you might find someone you work with who can help to broker the conversation.

It's always best to be prepared when you get ready to share your diagnosis at work. I like to think of this as a solution-focused approach even when there aren't any problems to solve. Think about your strengths and the things you struggle with: what do you want to highlight as things you might need more consideration with? You can figure out what adjustments you need and share these with your manager or your employer.

Think about what you do and don't want people to know. You get to control the narrative of how people talk about your autism and what your colleagues know about you. You don't have to share your autism diagnosis with your colleagues, but it can help to do this so that they know how to support you and what to do if unexpected situations come up that can throw you off.

## The positives of telling someone you're autistic

- You will always have someone to go to who understands you when you need to discuss being autistic or have someone to bounce ideas off for navigating the non-autistic world.
- It can prevent potential misunderstandings that may take place between you and your friends. If they know what the differences you have are, the support that you need in specific situations, and the signs that you aren't doing so well, they can help you. You won't be misunderstood if you've built that understanding together.
- Pretending to be something that you're not is exhausting. Sharing that part of yourself can stop that exhaustion; you're no longer keeping a secret about yourself.
- Telling friends is practice for all the other times you may need to share your autistic identity. This might be in romantic relationships, when making new friends, when talking to professionals, or when you share your diagnosis with your educators or employers.

## The negatives of telling someone you're autistic

To me, the positives of sharing your autistic identity far outweigh the negatives.

- You might have to contend with other people's misunderstanding of autism, but that does mean you get to tell them what autism is.

- You might face prejudice or discrimination, but that is the other person's issue, not yours. How they treat you says far more about them than it does about you. If you do experience prejudice or discrimination from someone because of being autistic, you can challenge it if you feel comfortable or have others challenge it if you do not.

Disclosure can be as long a journey as diagnosis itself. I promise you it is something you become comfortable with and find your way through.

# Part II

# Thriving while Autistic

# Mental Health and the Effect of Friends, the Environment, and the Importance of Support

Mental health is all about how we think (our brain), feel (our emotions), and act (what we do, influenced by our brain and emotions). Everybody has mental health: some have good mental health, some have not-so-good mental health, and others fluctuate between good and not-so-good mental health. The same is true for physical health and wellbeing – this oscillates and changes. We all have physical health and mental health; it can be a lifelong journey to take care of ourselves.

People often pit mental health and physical health against each other, using one to highlight struggles against some imagined hierarchy of suffering. You can see it in the 'battle' and 'warrior' language you often see around health. Our body and mind are imagined as a warzone, either at war with our very selves, each other, or society.

Mental health and physical health aren't more or less important than each other – they often go hand in hand, but unfortunately delayed access to healthcare, diagnosis and treatments is common for both types of health. Ideally, there would be a bit of equity, or, even more radically, justice within the health systems so that people could get the right care at the right time for as long as needed without financial obstacles. That might be a bit of a pipe dream, unfortunately.

Whether someone has good mental health, poor mental health, or a diagnosed and clinically managed mental health condition, they still experience a full range of emotions, thoughts, and feelings. When someone has better mental health, they might feel more confident in themselves, but this isn't always true. They might feel more positive, but this doesn't have to be all the time. It's not as clear-cut as we're made to think it is.

If someone has poorer mental health they might struggle with their thoughts, feelings, and actions – the components that make up their mental health. Emotions might be felt more strongly, or they might feel empty; things that brought joy might not bring joy any more. The things they used to do now take up much more mental and physical energy to do, and they might feel unable to control their feelings or actions.

None of this is linear either: there isn't one direction in which to be mentally well or mentally unwell; instead of a straight line between the two it's more of a messy squiggle, a journey of back and forth each hour and each day.

## Autism and our relationship with mental health

Mental (ill) health is increasingly a huge part of understanding autism but is by no means an inevitability of being autistic. Talking through what is and isn't normal for autistic people can help to destigmatize mental health conditions and our normal (or not) autistic expression. We aren't all inevitably anxious, depressed, and struggling with our mental health, but some things in life can encourage mental health conditions to develop.

For many people, autism assessment is based within the context of a mental health service. In the USA and the UK, autism is diagnosed by specialists, which can include nurses, psychiatrists, psychologists, or paediatricians. This is not because autism is a mental health condition, but because this is where diagnostic services have been commissioned or created. Psychiatry and psychology are the specialties within which understanding of autism has developed since professionals first started defining autism.

As autism is typically diagnosed within mental health services there are a few places where this could occur. These could be mental health outpatient services, adult autism services, mental health inpatient services, or private services. People are diagnosed by clinicians who are either publicly or privately funded depending on the resources available to them (their own finances) and the resources available in the healthcare system (staffing, autism services, and waiting times). Some of these aspects hold true in other countries and they all depend on the provision or focus of public and private healthcare services. Any route to diagnosis, as long as it is carried out by a qualified clinician, is valid, and if you self-identify that is also valid; each autism journey starts with a fair bit of self-exploration anyway.

Diagnosis can happen at any point in a person's life. Anything can happen to trigger a diagnosis. When we are younger it might be our parents, family, or teachers noticing that we aren't doing things in the same way as other children our age. For people who are diagnosed in adulthood, this might be through researching autism for themselves or by relating to representations of autism. It could also be through experiencing mental ill health, through the suggestion of medical professionals, or indeed for any reason that feels right for them.

Mental ill health and mental illness are not things you should expect to experience just because you are autistic. However, mental illness, as research shows, is something that is experienced by a high percentage of autistic people compared with non-autistic people. Research by Eaves and Ho (2008)[1] indicated

1    Eaves, L. C., & Ho, H. H. (2008). Young adult outcome of autism spectrum disorders. *Journal of Autism and Developmental Disorders, 38*(4), 739–747. https://doi.org/10.1007/s10803-007-0441-x

that 77 per cent of autistic young people they researched had a mental health condition. When you look at it like that the statistics are a little bit scary and disheartening: 77 is a big number. Although many autistic people experience mental illness, it isn't inevitable; it is something that could probably be avoided or reduced if the world included us better. Autism isn't necessarily the reason for mental illness – it correlates with but does not cause mental illness by itself.

In my case, my relationship with my mental health is tightly linked to how well I'm supported, how understanding and accepting people are of me as an autistic person, and generally whether things are certain or uncertain. Uncertainty and hypotheticals are my autistic kryptonite and research (un)fortunately tells me I am not alone: many autistic people find uncertainty is nearly impossible to tolerate.[2]

## Getting some help with your mental health

If you are struggling with your mental health or feel that you can't manage it alone, it is important to get the right help. You might want to start by speaking to family and friends that you trust about the difficulties you are experiencing. You don't have to make the big step of talking to a doctor first, you can make smaller steps like talking to family, friends, or strangers who work at mental health support charities. It can be scary; I know the scariness well.

You can talk to your general practitioner or primary care physician for advice, if that's what you want, or talk through your options, which might be a referral to mental health support services. Some services allow you to self-refer to mental health support, and you don't have to talk to your general

---

2    Boulter, C., Freeston, M., South, M., & Rodgers, J. (2014). Intolerance of uncertainty as a framework for understanding anxiety in children and adolescents with autism spectrum disorders. *Journal of Autism and Developmental Disorders, 44*(6), 1391–1402. https://doi.org/10.1007/s10803-013-2001-x

practitioner. There are many resources out there to help you plan what to say and what to make a note of when talking to a doctor.

You might want to tell your doctor or healthcare professional that you are autistic, so they make some reasonable adjustments or changes to your care. These adjustments could be:

- Communicating online or by email rather than talking on the phone. If they do have to use the phone, ask them to tell you a specific time that they will ring (and to stick to it).

- Ask for a 'what to expect' type document or walkthrough so you know what will happen, whom you might talk to, and when to expect different stages of the process. You are more than within your rights to know what to expect and to have this outlined for you.

- If appointments are in person, being able to manage the sensory environment so that it isn't overwhelming is important. This could mean changes to the lighting, and thinking about whether rooms and spaces are overly loud or if there are strong scents that linger.

- Figuring out where communication differences might be to try to avoid misunderstanding. I quite like using 'understanding check-ins' frequently so that my understanding is checked, and a clinician's understanding is checked (this is also called active or reflective listening). Sometimes it can feel as if saying 'Does that make sense?' or asking 'Can I repeat that to check I've understood you correctly?' is overkill or an imposition, but, you're entitled to have things make sense for you and to be understood by others.

- Having a friend, relative, or carer attend appointments with you (basically anyone you feel comfortable with). They can be there for a short time or the whole time. You might not want them there the whole time, maybe just for the beginning until you feel comfortable.

## Therapy or counselling

Your general practitioner may refer you for talking therapy, counselling, or a mental health service to assess the type of therapy best suited to your mental health need. You might choose to pursue private therapy, which is typically one-to-one and you choose the therapist based on their expertise and your needs (both mental health and financial). Different therapists are trained in different techniques and therapeutic ways of working, and shopping around and finding what works is an important part of therapy.

As autistic people we don't always get along with every type of therapy: some people do well with verbal forms of therapy and other people might do better with more abstract types of therapy like play or drama therapy. It's always a good thing to talk about being autistic and what this means for working with specific therapists or counsellors as they might need to adapt their work to meet your needs. A group of autistic and non-autistic people worked together to develop ideas for adapting therapy to meet autistic people's needs. The Authentistic Research Collective's guide provides many options for you to draw upon.[3]

### How to find a therapist in the UK

The mental health charity Mind offers lots of up-to-date information about finding a therapist and the different routes you can take in the UK. Depending on your needs there are different options open to you including general practitioner referral, self-referral, charitable support, and private paid therapy.

### Improving Access to Psychological Therapies (IAPT)

This is an NHS programme that you can self-refer to. IAPT offers talking therapy in a typically time-limited format, and

3   Stark, E., Ali, D., Ayre, A., Schneider, N., Parveen, S., Marais, K., Holmes, N., & Pender, R. (2021). *Psychological therapy for autistic adults.* Authentistic Research Collective. Retrieved 10 October 2022, from https://www.authentistic.uk

it aims to reduce barriers to accessing treatment or support. To find IAPT services near you, use the online 'IAPT service finder' on the NHS website.

### Accredited private therapists

If you are looking for a private therapist, you can look on counselling and psychotherapy websites or ask friends and family for recommendations. If you are looking online make sure that the counsellor or therapist you choose fits your needs and is accredited through a professional body. You're spending a lot of money, so you get to choose where it goes. It's best to be savvy with what you have rather than financially worse off without progress around your mental health.

### How to find a therapist in other countries

This is something I am very familiar with for the UK and less so for other countries. Often the approach is specific to each country, locality, or individual circumstance. The routes to support are not as simple as 'just talk to a doctor' might seem. The process might involve talking directly to psychiatry services by looking at which clinicians are funded by your healthcare provider, talking to a general practitioner, or seeking out a completely independent therapist. Any of these routes might be open to you, and some of them might be easier than others depending on the resources you have. What is most important is seeking a therapist who meets your needs, understands how to treat your mental health condition, and is someone you feel safe talking to.

## Medication

You might be prescribed medication to help manage or treat the condition you have. It is important to follow the instructions provided by the clinician who prescribes the medication. If you don't feel quite right or are experiencing side effects, talk to your doctor before reducing or stopping your medication. Often stopping psychiatric medication like antidepressants or psychotropic medicines can have even worse or more pronounced side effects. Always check the information provided alongside your medication for potential side effects that you could experience. You might also find some solidarity or ways to manage these side effects by reaching out to people on the same medication through forums or social media.

Any medication you are prescribed should have frequent medicine reviews to check that you are getting along with it and that it is doing what it is meant to do. These medications can take some time to start working so don't worry if you don't notice an impact in the first month or two. If you aren't getting along with a specific medication you can ask to change your medication. However, a doctor may want a specific period to elapse before trying new medication.

There is nothing wrong with needing medication for your mental health – it's necessary and is doing what your body doesn't do alone. We don't worry about medication helping our physical health conditions so we shouldn't worry about mental health medication helping us. Depending on their mental health condition, people might be on psychiatric medication for a short time or for a long time. Each experience is unique to you, your life, and your needs.

### Different kinds of antidepressants

The medication you are prescribed is likely to be antidepressants. Which specific antidepressant you will be offered will depend on any other conditions you have or medications you take. Antidepressants, ironically, aren't only prescribed to help manage depression, they're used for many different mental health conditions due to how they support our body's chemistry. With any of these medications, it is important that you take them as prescribed and tell your doctor about how they make you feel. Common antidepressants are:

- Selective serotonin reuptake inhibitors (SSRIs). These are the most widely prescribed antidepressants and have fewer side effects than many of the other types of antidepressants. SSRIs you might have heard of are fluoxetine (Prozac), citalopram (Celexa), and sertraline (Zoloft).

- Serotonin–noradrenaline reuptake inhibitors (SNRIs). These are like SSRIs: they both work to increase how much of a hormone is present in the brain. Some people respond better to SSRIs, while others respond better to SNRIs; this is figured out by trialling different antidepressants. Examples of SNRIs include duloxetine (Cymbalta) and venlafaxine (Effexor).
- Noradrenaline and specific serotonergic antidepressants (NASSAs). These might be used when people can't take SSRIs. They have similar side effects to SSRIs: people might experience drowsiness during the initial stage of taking NASSAs. A NASSA that might be prescribed is mirtazapine.
- Tricyclic antidepressants (TCAs). These aren't typically prescribed any more as there can be some dangers associated with TCAs if not taken correctly, and side effects can be more unpleasant. They might be used if someone doesn't respond to other antidepressants. Some types of TCAs are now used to treat things that aren't mental health conditions such as nerve pain.
- Monoamine oxidase inhibitors (MAOIs). These aren't generally prescribed any more and might only be prescribed in special circumstances as they have serious and highly impactful side effects and negatively interact with some medications.

## Autism and mental health conditions

Many mental health conditions frequently co-occur with autism, some of which might exist alongside being autistic and others that might be a misdiagnosis or partially overlap with autism. What is normal for the mental health of an autistic person might be different to what is normal for a non-autistic person. It can be difficult to figure out if someone's 'normal' is being seen as a mental health issue when it might not be a mental health issue at all.

For example, the sensory differences or the social struggles that autistic people experience might be seen as anxiety or social anxiety if viewed in addition to being autistic, or they might be seen as just part of being autistic. It all depends on perspective. Creating a firm line between 'this is autism' and 'this is another condition' can be difficult depending on what someone feels and how they are presenting.

Autism co-occurs with many mental health conditions, physical health conditions, and other types of neurodivergence. You might have one, some, or quite a few of these (I'm still finding out that my physical health issues and neurodivergence are a bit broader than I initially thought![4]). Each autistic person is different, and someone might have none, some, or a lot of these conditions that researchers, autistic people, and clinicians have found to co-occur alongside autism. Some of these are:

- anxiety or phobias
- depression
- eating disorders
- obsessive–compulsive disorder
- bipolar disorder
- borderline personality disorder/emotionally unstable personality disorder.

More research is constantly emerging about what treatments should be offered to autistic people and to figure out what mental health conditions we might have. The National Institute for Health and Care Excellence (NICE) is a UK organization that

---

4   I've collected more physical health conditions and neurodivergent conditions that I either didn't know I had or have developed as I've aged.

creates guidance for each health condition to describe how to recognize, assess, and treat the condition. For autism, there is some information and guidance about the adaptations that should be made when assessing and treating mental health conditions.[5] This guidance is specific to autism but is not specific to the range of mental health conditions that autistic people might experience. The work of NICE is similar to that of the National Institute for Mental Health (NIMH) or the World Health Organization (WHO) and provides information about different mental health conditions.

In this chapter, I use the guidance from NICE to talk through the steps for accessing support for different mental health conditions. The guidance isn't perfect but helps form a mental framework of what different options are. Unfortunately, the guidance might not match the reality of what you could experience while interacting with mental health services, as NICE guidance (and similar international guidance) presents an ideal that might not match the complexity of healthcare diagnosis and treatment.

I want to reiterate that I'm not a medical professional: I'm someone who has experienced and continues to experience mental ill health. This chapter outlines experiences of mental ill health that you might resonate with, but these experiences are not an inevitability for everyone. If you do resonate with or relate to some of the mental health symptoms outlined in this chapter you don't have to keep it to yourself. If you are worried about your mental health, please do talk to someone who can help you to access support. Reaching out for support is something that you can do at any point from when you first start to experience thoughts or feelings that worry you to when they are a persistent part of your life.

---

5    National Institute for Health and Care Excellence. (2009). Autism spectrum disorder in adults: diagnosis and management [CG142]. Retrieved 10 October 2022, from https://www.nice.org.uk/guidance/cg142/chapter/Recommendations#interventions-for-coexisting-mental-disorders

## Anxiety and phobias
### Anxiety

An anxiety disorder may manifest differently in autistic people compared with non-autistic people. Being anxious might seem inescapable in autism because who wouldn't be anxious in a world that doesn't naturally accommodate and support your autistic needs? Autistic people can have an intolerance of uncertainty, so when change happens we might find it more difficult to process that change. That lingering threat of uncertainty can cause anxiety.

### What does anxiety look like for autistic people?

Anxiety is often described as experiencing worry or panic; these worries become persistent and get to a level at which they overwhelm you so that you can no longer control them. An anxious person might be at any point on this anxiety journey. The physical feelings or symptoms of anxiety might be a racing heart rate/palpitations, shortness of breath, agitation, feelings of distress, shakiness, sweating, or nausea. I sometimes uncontrollably shiver or shake when very anxious, even in a very warm place. Anxiety doesn't always have any rhyme or reason. These might be difficult sensations to recognize or link to anxiety, especially if you struggle with understanding and processing your internal states, like in alexithymia, which is most easily described as difficulty with identifying and describing your emotions or bodily sensations.

Something I've seen described and have felt myself is having a bodily awareness of anxiety with all the physical symptoms, but this not translating to a cognitive awareness. This is something that can be common in autism, as you might physically feel anxious but not connect the physical manifestation to anxious thoughts. You might feel the anxious thoughts are your normal thinking style. Many of the times I've felt anxious or put in place remedies for future anxiety I did not think I was anxious; rather, I was doing the things I would always do. It was my norm; I didn't call it anxiety.

Anxiety, alongside the anxiety-related bodily sensations and thoughts, is also related to reassurance-seeking behaviours that enable you to feel in control of your anxiety or situation. These behaviours might include avoidance, adhering to routines without deviation, overpreparing for different eventualities, or seeking out reassurance from others. Some of these anxious behaviours might also be classed as autistic behaviours. This cross-over includes meltdowns, shutdowns, repetitive behaviours (stimming), leaving a situation if too overwhelmed, and 'obsessive' routines.

Not all behaviours associated with managing or redirecting anxiety are positive behaviours; some might include self-harm, isolation, and avoidance of situations. You can't technically become anxious if there aren't any demands or activities placed on you, but it isn't positive to disengage from everything either.

When you are an anxiously inclined person or someone with a diagnosed anxiety disorder, there might be specific situations or intangible experiences that can trigger anxiety. For autistic people these triggers might be demands or pressures, uncertainty or change, triggers from sensory overwhelm, anticipation of events that make them anxious, and social situations.

For some autistic people, the pressure and anxiety that a demand creates are linked to a 'profile' of autism called Pathological Demand Avoidance (PDA). An autistic person with PDA feels increased distress or anxiety caused by everyday demands. Avoiding the demands put on them by others and by life's expectations can be associated with anxiety and the impact of PDA can reach into every area of a person's life.

## Phobias

What are phobias?

Phobias fall under the broader category of anxiety but relate to a specific fear that someone has, which might be treated in different ways to other anxieties. A phobia might be a fear of a specific object, a place, a feeling, an animal, and many other things that a phobia can be constructed around. It's more than just a fear of something – it's an escalated and extreme level of fear. Someone who has a phobia has often shaped their life around avoiding the thing that they fear.

Phobias are generally split into two different categories, the first is *specific phobias*, which might just be related to things or situations that cause extreme fear or anxiety. The second is a *complex phobia*, in which there may be more things involved that give someone a deep-seated level of anxiety.

Complex phobias might seem easy to describe on the surface but are much more like icebergs in how they are shaped. The phobia that someone has might be much more interlinked to things that people might not be able to see. Agoraphobia (a phobia of being in situations that might be difficult to leave or escape from) is often simplified to a fear of leaving home or a fear of open spaces but is incredibly complex. A complex phobia might be linked to several triggers for that anxiety, and there might be several different aspects that feed into the continuation of fear.

### What might phobias mean for autistic people?

*Social phobia* or social anxiety is a complex phobia that is often oversimplified. It involves an intense and overwhelming fear of social situations, which shouldn't be dismissed as just awkwardness or shyness in social situations. It is a deeply rooted fear that can encompass someone's entire thoughts. People may conflate the social difficulty aspects of autism with social phobia or social anxiety.

Phobias related to the *sensory environment* like fear of sudden noises, flashing lights, unpleasant textures, or foods can be made worse by someone being hypersensitive to the sense or situation that causes the phobia.

*Phobias about situations*, particularly uncertain, new, or unpleasant sensations, might include visiting the dentist, going to school, visiting a new place, or going somewhere where something negative has happened. Sometimes these types of phobias are linked to traumatic experiences, for example, a situation like having a dental check-up or a specific dental practice.

Phobias concerning *parts of the body or bodily function* might be related to things like blood tests, injections, or vomiting. It is the build-up of fear before and surrounding the situation that can amplify anxiety. A phobia of vomiting has a specific name – emetophobia. Emetophobia can vary in severity, with triggers ranging from hearing someone being sick, seeing someone being sick, and fear of vomiting themselves, to fear of seeing vomit either as a physical object or even just written in a sentence.

Phobias relating to *animals or objects* might be associated with previous negative experiences. For some people, this might be a fear of dogs because they witnessed an aggressive dog, or they may fear a specific breed of dog. For others, it might be an intolerance of labels in clothes or exclusively wearing a specific type of clothing because it is the only thing that feels comfortable. Preferences can develop into avoidance and aversion to specific things, which maintains the anxiety.

Phobias can also relate to *specific patterns or visuals*. While some autistic people might be sensory seeking for specific visual patterns, others might have a debilitating fear of them (an example of this might be a fear of close holes or dots, which is called trypophobia). This can be more impactful for autistic people who are hypersensitive and who are unable to disengage easily from the thing that is causing the phobia.

### Coping and managing skills

Let someone know about your fears and worries! This could involve talking to friends, talking to family members, or reaching out to a doctor. It can be intimidating to share what you're worried about. However, if it is causing major disruption to your life then reaching out for help is the best thing to do. Sometimes, anxieties and phobias make sense. They can act to keep us well and alive but can also be terrible for us.

Medication

There isn't too much definitive research out there about which medications work well for autism and anxiety or phobias. Clinicians will prescribe what they know works well for anxiety and regularly monitor you to see if you have any negative side effects.

They might prescribe anti-anxiety medication or antidepressant medications; these might be taken daily or as needed. For some people, daily medication manages the base level of anxiety that they have; for others, as needed or 'pro re nata' (PRN) medication helps them as they can plan their medication around situations that make them anxious.

Therapy

Therapy for anxiety might be talking therapy or, if you have a specific phobia, you might be offered exposure therapy. Cognitive behavioural therapy (CBT) is a type of therapy that is commonly used in health services and has been proven to be highly effective in treating many conditions. Not every autistic person gets along with CBT so it is worth exploring CBT to see if it works for you and to see what adaptations you might need to therapy. If something doesn't work, you can push for changes to medication or therapy that meets your needs.

## Depression

In autistic people, depression commonly starts during adolescence and young adulthood, and can then continue during the rest of a person's life. Depression can be treated through multiple routes. Depression can often be episodic, which means it can happen in periods throughout your life.

Most people go through some periods of feeling down or sad. This is completely normal because no one can be happy absolutely all the time, but when you're depressed you feel persistently sad for weeks or months, rather than just a few days. That feeling of sadness might not even feel like sadness

– it might be an emptiness or a lack of happiness. Depression impacts people in different ways and the symptoms can range from mild to severe; these symptoms can also change from day to day and person to person.

## What is depression?

Depression is a mental health condition that impacts the way you think, feel, and act in a negative way. This means that it affects your thoughts, physical sensations, and behaviours. The thoughts, feelings, and actions that relate to depression are called symptoms of depression. Some of these are as follows.

### Emotions

Depression is characterized by low mood, meaning that there isn't as much happiness in what you are feeling as there might be for someone without depression. Depression is often viewed as feeling sad, but it is more than just sadness. It is complete hopelessness, feeling trapped in a cycle you don't have the energy to break, feeling empty of all emotions, feeling anxious or worried, and feeling irritated.

Depression isn't simply an absence of happiness or a focus on sadness that you can feel. It is an amplification of everything that might feel negative or a complete dulling of all emotions. Depression can weave its way into every part of you; it can take the confidence you once had and make you feel insecure and self-critical, or completely ruin your self-esteem. It slows your brain and makes you feel like you're trying to run through glue or as if a heavy cloud obscures the world around you. It's rough. Depression can look and feel different for different people and even for the same people at different points in their life.

Problems weigh heavily on your mind, but you can't gain the motivation to do even the simplest things to fix them. Solutions are never simple, but that doesn't matter when your mind feeds into this cycle of self-hatred and worthlessness.

Carrying the weight of everything that is wrong with the world can make you feel incredibly guilty: guilty that you're not doing more or feeling that you should be less of a burden (you're definitely not a burden) and so many spirals of guilt and shame.

### Physical and bodily sensations

Depression is often characterized as carrying around a heavy cloud that blocks out all happiness and joy. This 'cloud' can have a physical weight even if it is only metaphorical. It's a weight that disrupts your sleeping patterns, turning you into a nocturnal creature who might sleep during the day, someone who struggles to sleep enough, or someone who sleeps too much. Your circadian rhythm is completely knocked and sleep never feels restorative. Sleep becomes a way to stop the world for a bit, but this can leave you feeling tired all the time no matter how much sleep you get.

In turn, this means that no matter what you do you never have the energy to do things. These could be the things you used to enjoy or the things that are basic self-care like showering or changing your clothes. Everything feels like moving leaden limbs that your brain can't figure out how to operate.

Depression also affects your appetite: you might not want to eat because you don't feel hungry, or you might have an endless appetite. This can also cause changes in your weight and shape. Your body can physically hurt as much as you are mentally hurting with aches and pains that might not make sense.

### Actions

Someone with depression might act in ways to push others away, perhaps withdrawing from others by appearing oppositional, defiant, or aggressive. You may hurt yourself or think about hurting yourself. This could be through self-harming, suicidal ideation, or planning ways to hurt yourself or others. When depressed you might hurt on the inside and want to express this pain on the outside as well.

Things that you once found joy in like hobbies or interests might now be things you no longer want to spend time doing. This inability to find happiness in things that once brought joy is called anhedonia and is a hallmark of depression that can ripple out to education, work, family, and social circles, and cause disruption.

## What does depression look like for autistic people?

Depression is more common for autistic people and those with co-occurring conditions such as a learning disability or epilepsy. Research into how many autistic people there are with depression doesn't give us clear or exact figures. There are so many factors that feed into the wider picture of autism and depression. This means our age, ethnicity, sexuality, family experience, other conditions, traumatic events we've faced, and much more also have an impact on how likely we are to experience depression. What research can tell us is that depression is likely to impact autistic people from a young age, typically starting when we are teenagers or young adults and often persisting in episodes throughout our whole lives.

For autistic people, depression looks or feels different to how it looks or feels for non-autistic people. We show increased suicidal thoughts and ideation, or we might self-harm more as a way of self-managing our depression. Things that might be more associated with autism become more apparent. We can stim more or do more repetitive movements, and our social withdrawal in an attempt to shut out the world might be more obvious.

Some factors mean you might be more likely to experience depression, but the combination of these factors does not make depression inevitable. For example, if other members of your family currently have or in the past have experienced depression you might also experience depression – depression has some hereditary or genetic components. Events that cause upheaval in your life are linked to depression. These are events like bereavement, losing a job, being bullied, the end of a relationship, abuse, major traumatic illnesses, or changes to your health. We can experience some of these things more than non-autistic people.

Things like alexithymia or rumination, which autistic people experience more than non-autistic people, are also linked to depression. Alexithymia is being unable to describe or identify your internal feelings, which might mean feeling empty, confused, or sad. Rumination is the constant rehashing of or fixation on these negative thoughts or events.

### Getting help and support, and the impact of depression

Depression can be incredibly overwhelming when you're in the middle of it; it can feel like you're constantly sinking with no shoreline to swim to for safety. Depression is all-consuming. It draws you in, holds you tight, and attempts to crush you while convincing you that no one cares about you. It tells you that everyone hates you and that there is no escape.

My autism diagnosis came along during a crushing episode of depression. A psychiatrist noticed there was something more than depression and anxiety going on. I was already getting some support for the negativity that surrounded my every thought, but nothing seemed to shift until autism began to put everything into perspective. It didn't fix things, but it helped me to understand that the power I had to change my situation was greater than the power I had let others have over me.

### Asking others for help

Getting help when you are depressed can feel unjustly difficult as you are exposing yourself to being judged for the things you've tried to hide. Deciding to get help, whether you come to the decision by yourself or whether someone encourages you to do so, is a massive step. It is unfortunately followed by lots of other big steps. The first step is telling someone how you are feeling. That might be telling someone you know like a family member, friend, or a medical professional. This is so daunting because you might have to convince that person of your worthiness for help and support; it's a point of vulnerability that feels uncomfortable.

## Therapy and lifestyle changes

Based on how much depression is impacting your life and your ability to get on with 'everyday activities' your depression might be seen as mild, moderate, or severe. For severe depression, a doctor may suggest a combined approach of therapy and antidepressants. For mild depression, a doctor may suggest lifestyle changes and self-directed support to aid recovery. Recovery is not a linear route from depressed to 'normal' – you might move through different treatments and supports as your experience of depression progresses.

Lifestyle changes include allowing yourself more time to do things without being harsh on yourself, spending more time with others, and exercise. Exercise can be as basic as going for a walk; it doesn't have to be an intensive team sport. Self-help techniques aren't guaranteed to magically cure depression, and it can feel frustrating when they are suggested to you over and over. While they're not a fix-all, they can be used to build healthy mental wellbeing habits.

## Eating disorders
### What are eating disorders?

An eating disorder is when you have an unhealthy attitude towards or a disordered relationship with food, your weight or shape, and eating. Eating disorders have a huge impact on your life and your health and have a lasting impact on your body. Eating disorders have the highest mortality rate of all mental health conditions. There are a few different types of eating disorder.

Anorexia is restricting calorie intake through multiple means and increasing methods to burn calories. Bulimia involves increasing calorie intake and then using measures such as exercise, medicine, or vomiting to stop weight gain. Eating disorders revolve around food and control, which could be eating too much or eating too little, and how you become obsessed with your weight (the numbers) and your body shape (how those numbers relate to the shape of your body). The obsession with weight and shape cannot be disengaged from; the thoughts and actions consume the person.

Anyone can develop an eating disorder; they typically start in adolescence and continue throughout a person's whole life. People can recover from their eating disorder but will battle the 'gremlins' that try to bring them back into that mindset with every meal and trigger for their eating disordered habits. Men, women, and those who don't identify as either can develop an eating disorder – mental health doesn't discriminate.

As I don't have personal experience with eating disorders, I can't speak to how they feel internally. I can only write about the autistic people I have supported with eating disorders and what they have asked for in that support. Many people have described much better than I can what being autistic and having an eating disorder is like. Some have written blogs, books, and created graphics or videos about autism and eating disorders.[6] Please do engage with others who have personal experience of autism and eating disorders to truly understand what this experience is like, but don't ask someone unless they are comfortable talking about it.

### Anorexia nervosa or anorexia

If you suffer from this mental health condition, you might utilize multiple ways to keep your weight low or to a number

---

6   A book I read by an autistic person who has experience with eating disorders helped inform some of how I think about autism and eating disorders. As a note of caution, vomiting, trauma, depression, suicidality, and restricted eating are discussed, so if you do want to read it, be prepared for this. Charlotte Amelia Poe's memoir *How To Be Autistic* tells their story of growing up and not quite fitting in.

that you choose. Anorexic people try to achieve a low weight by reducing their intake of food and by burning calories by obsessively exercising. People with anorexia use multiple strategies to lower their weight and change their body shape to their perceived ideal. Anorexia is the deadliest of all mental health conditions due to the devastating impacts it has on a person's body and mind; many people die through malnutrition or complications due to malnutrition or starvation, or by suicide.

### Bulimia nervosa

Bulimia shares some symptoms or characteristics with anorexia but presents differently. While there might be some calorie restriction in bulimia, it is typically characterized by consuming a lot of food in a short amount of time and then eliminating those calories deliberately, through methods to remove the food from your body. While anorexia is focused on restriction, bulimia has traditionally been characterized as cycles of 'binging' and 'purging'.

### Binge eating disorder

This condition is similar to bulimia as it involves consuming lots of food in a short space of time but differs in some of the associated behaviours.

### Avoidant Restrictive Food Intake Disorder

Avoidant Restrictive Food Intake Disorder (ARFID) is an eating disorder that is like anorexia as it too involves the extreme restriction of food that is eaten or consumed. However, with ARFID there isn't the same focus or concern with weight, body shape, or size.

### Other Specified Feeding or Eating Disorder

Other Specified Feeding or Eating Disorder (OSFED) is an eating disorder that doesn't fit neatly into the label of an alternative eating disorder. Someone with OSFED might have symptoms of anorexia or bulimia or of binge eating disorder. Although it isn't clearly a single eating disorder, it is still a serious condition.

## Symptoms of an eating disorder

The *mental symptoms* of an eating disorder often focus on things like worrying about your weight and shape. It can consume all or most of your thoughts and is difficult to stop thinking about. You might avoid social situations or spaces that revolve around food such as dinners with friends or family, cafés, restaurants, social situations that take place at mealtimes, and anywhere that food could be prepared or eaten. You may also have incredibly strict routines around everything to do with food. You may have a disordered relationship with the amount of food that you eat, either not eating enough to sustain yourself or eating too much food. You might have feelings of being withdrawn from others, feeling misunderstood by others, feeling anxious, or feeling depressed all or most of the time.

The *physical symptoms* related to eating disorders get worse as your eating disorder develops. Many are linked to starvation or your body having to work without the nutrients and energy it needs. These include hair loss, developing lanugo[7] (if you have anorexia), dizziness, fainting, exhaustion, and hallucinations. You may also experience sore joints, disruptions to menstruation (if you have periods), digestive issues, feeling cold, and sensations linked to anxiety.

## What do eating disorders look like for autistic people?

Research has shown that autistic people, particularly autistic women, make up a larger-than-expected percentage of people with anorexia. There is a growing area of research that highlights this intersection of autism and eating disorders. This has

---

7   Lanugo is soft, downy hair typically covering infants in their early period of life. When present beyond infancy lanugo is often a sign that someone is struggling to regulate their body temperature.

been supported by autistic women with anorexia discussing their experiences of the condition and anorexia treatment.[8] For autistic people, the experience of an eating disorder might be different to that of non-autistic people, and the motivations behind it might be different.

You might not feel or process a sense of hunger in the same way a non-autistic person does; this can be due to alexithymia. You may develop sensory aversions to specific foods based on textures, smells, tastes, or how they sound when you eat them. You might have rules that you develop around food that can lead to routines which become too rigid for you to change as they reflect a sense of safety. These rules or routines can form around food, mealtimes, and food preparation. Ultimately, an eating disorder for an autistic person might not be as strongly connected to weight, shape, or body image as it is for 'traditional' experiences of eating disorders.

## Getting help and support

If you are worried you have an eating disorder, please visit your general practitioner and ask for support. You can access help by speaking to those that know if you feel comfortable doing so, or by speaking to people who are knowledgeable about eating disorders. Some eating disorder charities offer specific spaces online to talk to others at any point in your eating disorder journey. The staff members who provide help through charities are trained to offer some of the support you may need but are not a substitute for clinical support from a doctor or eating disorder service.

---

8   Babb, C., Brede, J., Jones, C. R., Elliott, M., Zanker, C., Tchanturia, K., Serpell, L., Mandy, W., & Fox, J. R. (2021). 'It's not that they don't want to access the support... it's the impact of the autism': the experience of eating disorder services from the perspective of autistic women, parents and healthcare professionals. *Autism*, 25(5), 1409–1421. https://doi.org/10.1177/1362361321991257

## Therapy for eating disorders

There are some suggested treatments for any person with an eating disorder; however, currently, there isn't evidence-based guidance for what works specifically for autistic people with an eating disorder. That being said, research is making progress to find what works best and what should be commissioned. Current practice suggests that eating disorders should be treated with talking therapies such as cognitive behavioural therapy enhanced (CBT-E) in conjunction with medication, but not medication on its own. Based on what eating disorder you have and what your clinician decides you might have individual therapy, group therapy, or self-directed therapy.

As with any psychological therapy, it is important that you ask for adaptations and that those helping you know that you are autistic. If they know you are autistic and what your needs are they can tailor their approach to you. When you receive treatment for your eating disorder, support will target how the eating disorder has impacted your body, your mind, and your daily life. Treatment works around the physical damage that your eating disorder has caused to your body, redeveloping your relationship with food, and figuring out new routines that are less pressured around food and exercise.[9]

## Obsessive-compulsive disorder
### What is obsessive-compulsive disorder?

Obsessive-compulsive disorder (OCD) is a mental health condition characterized by obsessive thoughts and compulsive behaviours. Having OCD is upsetting for the person who has the condition, exhausting to deal with, and can get in the way of their everyday life. It is upsetting for those around you who

---

9    *The Eating Disorder Recovery Journal* is a great book by Cara Lisette, who is herself in recovery from an eating disorder, and may provide some support to you if you are struggling with an eating disorder and are going through your own recovery. *The Eating Disorder Recovery Journal* offers activities that Cara has utilized during her recovery.

support you as they feel helpless to support you to manage your obsessions or compulsions. Treatment is a key component of helping you to manage the thoughts and behaviours associated with OCD. OCD consists of two components: obsessions and compulsions.

- Obsessions are intrusive or otherwise unwelcome thoughts. These thoughts can be words, images, urges, doubts, or fears that can be difficult to remove focus from. They emerge or intrude over and over. Obsessions force you to feel anxious due to the content of the thoughts and how these link to other aspects of your life.
- Compulsions are actions that you take; these might be enacting the obsessive thoughts you have. Compulsions might be repetitive things you do to reduce anxious or obsessive thoughts. Not all compulsions are repeating actions, as media stereotypes of OCD often portray. They are things you feel you must do to prevent negative events from occurring or actions that help you feel safe.

OCD can impact anyone, regardless of gender or age. Typically, OCD begins in adolescence or early adulthood and persists for the rest of someone's life. OCD can be managed through therapy, medication, and coping mechanisms.

## What does OCD look like for autistic people?

First and foremost, many people don't find positives in OCD but do find good parts in being autistic. OCD comes with unwanted intrusive thoughts, obsessions, and compulsions that can make life incredibly difficult. There are some overlaps between autistic and OCD behaviours, but these don't have the same motivations.

In some cases, OCD might be mistaken for autism or autism mistaken for OCD if someone does not know the context behind someone's actions. Some of these cross-over or mistaken behaviours are:

- Compulsion-like behaviours in autism such as needing to touch a sensorily pleasing fabric, stimming, or repeating a phrase. What appears to be a compulsion might be an impulsive or otherwise soothing behaviour.
- Restrictive or repetitive behaviours like stimming in autism or checking objects or scenarios in OCD (e.g. checking a door is locked).
- Using routines to guide your daily life. Autistic people enjoy the structure and safety of routines and people with OCD may also utilize strict routines, but the intent is different.
- Not enjoying change because it is upsetting. Both autistic people and those with OCD can find change challenging but may have different reasons behind why this is the case.
- Ritual-like behaviour. For example, I make my cups of tea in the same way each time because that is how I know they will taste good to me. However, I don't associate this ritual with anything negative; if I pour in a bit too much milk it just means milky tea, not a catastrophe.
- Restricted interests, which might be special interests for autistic people, and for those with OCD might be 'safe' thinking patterns.

Our autistic actions mean something different when viewed through an OCD lens. I pull on my fingers without rhythm when anxious to ground myself, which is an anxious stim. I don't have a set amount that 'I have to do'. If someone with OCD did the same thing it might still be related to anxiety or might be a compulsion with fixed patterns or connections to preventing negative consequences. It is easy to see how autistic behaviours can be misconstrued as OCD behaviours.

For someone who is autistic and has OCD, some of their OCD symptoms might not be recognized as fully as they should be. Unfortunately, diagnostic overshadowing means that a diagnosis of OCD can happen more slowly if a clinician focuses on someone's autism diagnosis or attributes distressing experiences to autism rather than OCD.

## Getting support for your OCD

If you are worried about intrusive thoughts, obsessions, or compulsive actions you carry out to prevent bad things from happening, you should speak to someone you trust about these worries. This might be a friend or a family member or your general practitioner. Your general practitioner will listen to your concerns and refer you to a mental health service for an assessment. If you fit the criteria for OCD this opens up treatment options like specific therapies, medication, and pathways for treatment. Asking for help is the first step to creating a treatment or management plan that works for you.

### Therapy for OCD

Therapy options aren't specific to treating OCD in autistic people but can be adapted to your needs. There are two types of therapy that you might be offered to support you with OCD.

- CBT is proven to be highly effective in treating OCD. CBT offers those with OCD alternative beliefs to replace the negative intrusive thoughts that form part of their OCD thought patterns.
- Exposure therapy and response prevention might be used to encourage people with OCD to experience the things that cause their OCD-related anxiety. It works to help you to tolerate or respond to these anxieties without using your compulsions.

## Medication

It is recommended that SSRIs are used to support the treatment of OCD in adults. Medication is one option that a clinician may discuss with you: some people find that medication supports them alongside therapy and beyond for managing their OCD, while others may not want medication. You can discuss with your clinician what treatment plan best fits your needs, the potential benefits of different types of treatment types alone or combined, and if you want to make any changes at any point.

### Further reading on OCD

As someone who does not have lived experience of OCD, I have found reading the work of others, both those with lived experience of OCD[10] and those who research or work in OCD,[11] to be useful in developing my understanding. If you think you are experiencing OCD reading the work of those who write about their own experience of OCD may offer something you resonate with.

### Bipolar disorder

Bipolar disorder is a mental health condition that impacts how you feel and in turn impacts how you act. Bipolar disorder is often characterized as 'swinging' between depression or low mood and being excitable or having high energy. You may have heard the term mania used to describe the experiences associated with being excitable or having high energy in bipolar disorder.

Research has shown that some autistic people experience

---

10   Marianne Eloise is an autistic writer who published on this intersection between autism and OCD in her book *Obsessive, Intrusive, Magical Thinking*, which details how these different types of fixations can manifest.
11   Yuhas, D. (2019, 27 February). Untangling the ties between autism and obsessive-compulsive disorder. Spectrum. Retrieved 11 October 2022, from https://www.spectrumnews.org/features/deep-dive/untangling-ties-autism-obsessive-compulsive-disorder

bipolar disorder, but we don't know how much these two conditions co-occur. What we do know comes from clinicians' experiences of treating bipolar disorder in autistic people and from autistic people themselves who talk about experiences of bipolar disorder. Both autism and bipolar disorder are lifelong conditions that should be supported throughout a person's life. Autism is supported through reasonable adjustments and putting in place support for someone's access needs. Bipolar disorder is treated or managed through medication, therapy, and support services.

### What is bipolar disorder?

As a condition bipolar disorder develops in later adolescence and continues for the rest of a person's life. It doesn't normally start after the age of 40. Anyone can develop bipolar disorder; it is not more likely for any gender or background. Researchers don't know the exact causes of bipolar disorder, but they have identified some potential triggers. These triggers combine inherited and environmental factors. Examples include having a family member who has bipolar disorder and experiencing extreme life stress (debt, grief, insecure housing, trauma). Many factors can feed into the development of bipolar disorder, which makes figuring out specific causes or pathways difficult.

There are many different symptoms that someone who has bipolar disorder might experience. These symptoms include:

- Periods or episodes of mania. Longer episodes of mania might include feeling happy/euphoric, having lots of energy, making impulsive decisions, becoming irritated easily, and talking quickly.
- Hypomanic episodes are like mania but are shorter in duration.
- Periods or episodes of depression.
- Episodes of mixed mania and depression.

These periods or episodes can cycle through mania and depression, with a break in the middle in which you might feel like your normal self. Sometimes you don't get a break; this is called rapid cycling and involves faster switching between mania and depression.

### What does bipolar disorder look like for autistic people?

Bipolar disorder impacts your everyday life. You might experience mood swings that can feel exhausting and impact your relationships, hobbies, education, or employment. You might have difficulty sleeping or struggle with eating. You might be easily irritated and hypersensitive to the world around you or the actions of others, which might amplify existing autistic sensitivities.

Bipolar disorder may also make it difficult to understand and process your internal feelings. You may experience stronger suicidal thoughts or desires to self-harm when in periods of depression. Experiencing symptoms of bipolar disorder alongside being autistic can be incredibly distressing because of the impact on your behaviour and mood. Often the decisions made during episodes of mania have consequences that must be managed outside of these periods. Examples include buying expensive items, negative actions towards friends or family members, plans made, or other consequences for actions made by your manic self.

Some experiences or symptoms of bipolar disorder might be overlooked in people with an autism diagnosis due to diagnostic overshadowing as some symptoms of bipolar disorder may appear akin to autistic behaviour.

### Getting help and support for bipolar disorder

If you feel as if some of your experiences of the world are not autism but might be symptomatic of bipolar disorder, you must talk to family, friends, someone you trust, or your general practitioner. Autism cannot be treated but bipolar disorder can.

Your general practitioner will be able to discuss your

concerns with you and refer you to services to get support with your mental health and the impacts that bipolar disorder is having on your life. The local mental health service will be able to tailor support to your needs based on key components of your experience of bipolar disorder. They will triage your needs through routine questionnaires, by talking to you, or by taking a history of your life as it relates to bipolar disorder. These questions will figure out if bipolar disorder fits with your experience as a diagnostic label and what treatment options will work best.

A specialist psychiatrist will make a diagnosis of bipolar disorder based on your presentation of symptoms, family history, the impact your symptoms have on your life, and observation of how your symptoms impact you over time. It can be quite a lengthy process from initially raising concerns through to diagnosis. A prolonged period before diagnosis means that clinicians can observe you for longer to make sure that bipolar disorder is the right diagnosis for you. They want to get this right as the diagnosis impacts other areas of your life. For example, people with bipolar disorder must inform the driver licensing and registration body for their country (in the UK this is the DVLA or the DMV in America) as bipolar disorder can impact your ability to drive safely.

Bipolar disorder is a highly stigmatized mental health disorder as the behaviours and ways of expressing yourself can be viewed as negatively impacting the lives of those around you. Bipolar disorder should not be stigmatized, and you should be supported by those around you.

## Treatment for bipolar disorder

As with other mental health conditions, there isn't specific guidance for assessing, treating, and supporting autistic people with bipolar disorder. Although we know that these two conditions co-occur, finding specific treatments that support all needs is difficult.

Typical treatment for bipolar disorder involves combining

medication and psychological therapies. You can find the right combination of medication and therapy for you by working through the options available locally with your clinical team. There may also be some lifestyle support to help manage some of the consequential aspects of bipolar disorder. These could be things like housing, money management, employment support services, and support with access to education.

### Medication for bipolar disorder

Prescribed medications include antipsychotic medications or mood stabilizers. These medications are intended for long-term use as bipolar disorder is a lifelong condition that needs lifelong management. The medication you are prescribed may have side effects that you need to be aware of, and you should notify your doctors if they occur. Your medication should be reviewed frequently with your psychiatrist to ensure that it is having a positive impact and that negative impacts are controlled.

### Therapy for bipolar disorder

There are a two pathways to therapy that are used in a community mental health setting: at an outpatient mental health service, or as part of inpatient mental health services. The therapy offered may include:

- Psychoeducation, which involves finding out more about bipolar disorder, what it is, and what can make it worse. The aim of psychoeducation is to enable you to better understand your condition and how you can put in place lifestyle changes that support you. Psychoeducation intends to empower people to self-manage their conditions and is a patient-mediated intervention rather than doctor-led.
- CBT can be used to support you during the episodes of depression that you experience due to bipolar disorder. CBT aims to challenge your thoughts, feelings, and behaviours.

## Borderline personality disorder or emotionally unstable personality disorder

Research shows that there is some overlap between personality disorders and autism;[12] many autistic people are often diagnosed or misdiagnosed with a personality disorder before they receive their autism diagnosis.[13] Personality disorders are unfortunately highly stigmatized and misunderstood conditions. The negative understanding of personality disorders mirrors the damaging framing by professionals that autism has gone through. A lot of the writing about borderline personality disorder (BPD) and personality disorders in general can be difficult to read as the label has been used to place a lot of shame and hatred on people who have been diagnosed with the condition.

### What is BPD/emotionally unstable personality disorder?

BPD is characterized by 'disturbed patterns of thought and behaviour' and difficulty with emotions and relationships. According to the DSM-5 (2013), some BPD symptoms start in early adulthood and are seen in multiple contexts of your daily life. These are:

- avoiding real or imagined abandonment
- emotional instability or dysregulation
- impulsive behaviour
- patterns of intense but unstable relationships with others
- disturbed sense of self or unstable self-image
- suicidal behaviour and self-harm
- dissociation

12  Dudas, R. B., Lovejoy, C., Cassidy, S., Allison, C., Smith, P., & Baron-Cohen, S. (2017). The overlap between autistic spectrum conditions and borderline personality disorder. *PLoS One, 12*(9), e0184447. https://doi.org/10.1371/journal.pone.0184447
13  Vegni, N., D'Ardia, C., & Torregiani, G. (2021). Empathy, mentalization, and theory of mind in borderline personality disorder: possible overlap with autism spectrum disorders. *Frontiers in Psychology, 12*. https://doi.org/10.3389/fpsyg.2021.626353

- chronic feelings of emptiness
- strong feelings of anger.

Emotional dysregulation or instability is one of the main symptoms that impacts the daily life of people with BPD. The symptoms of a personality disorder may range from mild to severe and continue throughout someone's life.

## Issues with personality disorder as a label

The UK mental health charity Mind[14] explains some of the issues and controversies around personality disorders well. Often the emotions, thoughts, and behaviours that are categorized as belonging to a personality disorder are the appropriate reaction to going through difficult and traumatic life experiences. These reactions are often pathologized (negatively over-medicalized) through personality disorder labels that don't actually fit people's lived experiences.

For some people, the diagnosis may help them to access treatment, and for others, the label of 'personality disorder' might be something they don't wish to have. This is due to how the label negatively impacts their navigation of the health system and leads to a focus on fixing them rather than the issues in their life. Focusing on supporting someone with the external things they find difficult in life might be better than 'fixing' the individual. This could be through support in finding employment, managing money, or maintaining healthy relationships.

I've met people on both sides of this: those who didn't like the impact of the label on them and those who utilized the label as part of their access to treatment. It isn't a clean or linear spectrum for anyone who interacts with the 'BPD industrial complex'. It is a personal journey to find out what benefits and

---

14 Mind. (2020). Personality disorders: why is it controversial?. Retrieved 29 June 2022, from https://www.mind.org.uk/information-support/ types-of-mental-health-problems/personality-disorders/ why-is-it-controversial

consequences there are to a highly controversial label. I'm far from qualified to say much about what personality disorders are like to live with. I'll try to focus on treatments and support while acknowledging there are delicate aspects to this diagnosis.

## BPD and autism

There are some shared experiences that autistic people and people with BPD may have, particularly around sense of self, relationships with others, and emotions. Megan Anna Neff, an autistic therapist, talks about where these two conditions cross over and more on their Neurodivergent Insights blog.[15]

## How is BPD treated?

Treatment for BPD usually involves a type of psychotherapy. The therapy aims to help you get a better understanding of how you think and feel. This could be by talking through scenarios or emotions with a therapist or using more creative ways of working through situations with a therapist. As a primary feature of BPD is emotional instability or dysregulation, the therapy to treat BPD often focuses on giving you a sense of control over your thoughts and feelings.

Any psychotherapy for BPD must be carried out by someone who is trained to work with people who have BPD. There might be more than one mental health professional involved in your care as clinicians often have different specialities or roles within a team. The clinicians who work with you must not hold stigmatizing views about personality disorders. They should be focused on supporting you as a whole individual.

### Psychotherapy for BPD

The psychotherapy that you choose to help treat your BPD might be based on your research, what is available in your

---

15 Neff, M. (2021). Borderline personality disorder or autism — insights of a neurodivergent clinician. Retrieved 29 June 2022, from https://neurodivergentinsights.com/misdiagnosis-monday/boderline-personality-disorder-or-autism

local area, or your preference based on previous experience. Treatment for BPD is long term, which can mean therapy for a year or longer. Therapy should be person centred (tailored to your needs).

You might be offered Dialectical Behaviour Therapy (DBT) or Mentalization-Based Therapy (MBT).

DBT is a therapy specifically designed to treat BPD. It derives from two key factors that relate to BPD. These are that people with BPD are emotionally vulnerable and that people with BPD grow up in an environment that is dismissive of their thoughts and feelings. DBT tries to break the vicious and self-perpetuating cycle that these two factors create. This is done by validating your feelings, not dismissing them, and by utilizing dialectics. Dialectics teaches us that the world isn't simple and that many views and opinions exist – the multitude of views might support or contradict our own views.

MBT is used to tackle an idea that researchers have associated with BPD. Researchers have hypothesized that people with BPD have a worsened capacity to mentalize (thinking about thinking). MBT tries to build these skills by getting you to think about your thoughts and ideas. You then assess and judge these thoughts for how useful they are to you. Are the thoughts realistic and are they based in reality? By building these skills you are enabled to understand the impact of your thoughts and others' thoughts about you or the world.

Medicine

Medicine isn't usually suggested for BPD itself; it might be used to treat other mental or physical health conditions that someone has alongside BPD. Mood stabilizers or antipsychotic medication are sometimes prescribed to help with mood swings or reduce the impulsive behaviour that might occur with BPD. As always, medication is something you should discuss with your clinician to assess the benefits, potential challenges, and suitability for you.

# Autism and Physical (III) Health

As an autistic person I've realized that many people aren't just autistic – we tend to be autistic *and* something else. This 'and' is generally another neurodivergent condition or mental health condition, but there are many physical health conditions that are known to co-occur alongside autism. You might be autistic, but you might also be autistic with a physical health condition added on top. Managing being autistic in an unaccommodating world is a lot to deal with, never mind additional mental and physical health conditions.

For me, this means I'm an autistic person, I've managed depression in my past, and anxiety is something I struggle with every day alongside multiple chronic illnesses. Thinking about physical health and how it interacts with autistic identity *is* incredibly important, in my view at least. Autism shapes so much of our daily experience and perception of the world. When you add on different health conditions that can make daily life more difficult to manage. Difficult, mainly because it means managing your sensory experiences, social expectations, anxieties, and processing what is going on – all alongside physical health conditions which can make any of those systems harder.

Being autistic not only impacts physical and mental health conditions but also impacts our access to diagnosis and treatment of these health conditions. If your communication needs mean that you struggle with talking on the phone or can't articulate your symptoms in a way that a clinician understands, your healthcare is impacted. If you become overwhelmed by the sensory and social pressures of seeking support, your access to healthcare is impacted. Researchers have amplified this by talking to autistic people about the things we struggle with when it comes to healthcare.[1] They've unfortunately also looked at how much sooner we die – often of preventable or avoidable causes.

It isn't all doom and gloom, although some days it can feel that way. Just as we can find a supportive community of autistic people to share in our similarities and differences, we can do the same for our physical health conditions. Being autistic is not the end of the world, and nor are the physical health conditions you might have.

## So, what physical health conditions do autistic people have?

Autistic people are more likely to have quite a few physical health conditions alongside being autistic. Some of these are genetic or hereditary so are often seen in families. This means a family member might have the same condition as you or a similar condition. Different health conditions that autistic people might have fit into a few different categories:

- *Neurological conditions* and central nervous system (CNS) differences impact the brain. Epilepsy is a neurological condition that is incredibly common within autism as roughly 12 per cent of autistic people have epilepsy and about 6 per cent of people who have epilepsy are autistic.[2]

1   Doherty, M., Neilson, S., O'Sullivan, J., Carravallah, L., Johnson, M., Cullen, W., & Shaw, S. C. (2022). Barriers to healthcare and self-reported adverse outcomes for autistic adults: a cross-sectional study. *BMJ Open, 12*(2), e056904. doi:10.1136/bmjopen-2021-056904
2   Autistica. (2019). Epilepsy – Autism. Retrieved 29 June 2022, from https://www.autistica.org.uk/what-is-autism/signs-and-symptoms/epilepsy-and-autism

- *Cardiovascular conditions* impact the heart and the blood vessels. For autistic people this might be postural orthostatic tachycardia syndrome (POTS), which is a higher-than-normal increase in heart rate (tachycardia) that occurs after sitting up or while standing (postural orthostatic). People may also feel dizzy or faint.
- *Gastrointestinal conditions* are illnesses that can impact any part of your gastrointestinal system. This is essentially anywhere along the route food takes in your body. These conditions include gastroesophageal reflux disease (GERD or GORD), irritable bowel syndrome (IBS), and inflammatory bowel disease (IBD). This could be reflux and nausea in your throat or stomach, food allergies or intolerances, abdominal pains, and any disruption on the way out like constipation or diarrhoea.
- *Connective tissue disorders* are conditions that impact the tissues that hold our bodies together in our skin, bones, blood vessels, joints, and tendons. They are autoimmune conditions that impact the structure and strength of your connective tissue, for example, Ehlers Danlos syndrome (EDS) or inflammatory connective tissue disorders like arthritis.
- *Metabolic conditions* and diabetes relate to how food and energy are processed inside your body. This could mean becoming overweight or having conditions like Type 1 or Type 2 diabetes. Autistic teenagers and young adults are about three times more likely than non-autistic people to develop Type 2 diabetes.[3]
- *Pulmonary and respiratory conditions* impact your breathing, including your throat and your lungs. These conditions include asthma and chronic obstructive pulmonary disease (COPD). Autistic people and those

---

3   Schott, W., Tao, S., & Shea, L. (2022). Co-occurring conditions and racial-ethnic disparities: Medicaid enrolled adults on the autism spectrum. *Autism Research, 15*(1), 70–85. https://doi.org/10.1002/aur.2644

with other developmental disabilities are twice as likely to have asthma compared to non-autistic people.[4]

- Autistic people can experience changes and disruptions to *puberty*. This could be early or delayed puberty, or changes in what puberty looks like. Early puberty is something experienced by many autistic girls.[5] Puberty has a life-changing impact on autistic children and teenagers.[6]
- Autistic people can also struggle with *sleep and energy*. We can experience sleep disturbances such as insomnia and reduced energy capacities linked to chronic fatigue syndrome, myalgic encephalomyelitis, and burnout.

This may sound like a tidal wave of potential health woes that every autistic person will have but, as with anything, these are all a maybe, a probability percentage. Maybe autistic people will experience some of these health conditions but not all of them. The message I'm trying to get across is that autistic people experience a huge range of co-occurring health conditions that can impact any system of the body. Unfortunately, doctors haven't connected these dots yet.

If you start spending more time around other autistic people, the realization of 'I do that too' moves from autism-specific things to a range of physical and mental health conditions. It's one of the reasons meeting people like you is so important. It helps lead to recognition and awareness of your own normal.

---

4    Xie, L., Gelfand, A., Delclos, G. L., Atem, F. D., Kohl, H. W., & Messiah, S. E. (2020). Estimated prevalence of asthma in US children with developmental disabilities. *JAMA Network Open*, *3*(6), e207728–e207728. https://doi.org/10.1001/jamanetworkopen.2020.7728

5    Corbett, B. A., Vandekar, S., Muscatello, R. A., & Tanguturi, Y. (2020). Pubertal timing during early adolescence: advanced pubertal onset in females with autism spectrum disorder. *Autism*, *13*(12), 2202–2215. https://doi.org/10.1002/aur.2406

6    Opar, A. (2021, 24 March). Puberty and autism: An unexplored transition. Spectrum. Retrieved 29 June 2022, from https://www.spectrumnews. org/features/deep-dive/puberty-and-autism-an-unexplored-transition

## Accessing healthcare that meets your needs

There are some scary statistics about autism and the disparities in our physical health, mental health, healthcare access,
and our mortality. This is generally a result of autistic communication differences not being understood or supported.
In turn, healthcare systems are generally inaccessible. Adding
to that, the connection of co-occurring health conditions with
autism has not happened sufficiently to support these conditions properly. Our differences mean that it can be harder
to talk to healthcare professionals about our health needs,
and these needs are often not understood. Research into the
health conditions we have alongside autism hasn't caught up
to our lived realities but is starting to. It is not the fault of
autistic people that our experiences with healthcare are often
worse than those of non-autistic people. The fault lies within
an inflexible system that has not listened to or appreciated
the needs we have.

An example of this might be the differences that autistic
people have in expressive communication. If someone is in
pain, they are expected to express that through screaming,
a pained facial expression, recoiling when sore areas are
touched, crying, or verbalizing where the pain is and what
it feels like. An autistic person may not show these signs of
pain. They might struggle to verbalize their pain in a way that
healthcare professionals understand, for example, by categorizing it on a pain chart. Healthcare specialists expect us to talk
about 'stinging', 'burning', 'throbbing', or 'dull' sensations, the
strength of the pain, or how it makes us feel. You can't describe
that if you're not sure of anything other than 'this really hurts'.

Alternative descriptors for pain that provide more contex-
tual cues and clarity as to what pain descriptors mean enable
autistic people to better describe our pain. Reworking the
descriptors enables us to be understood by those asking about
our pain. Crossed communication wires like these are a classic
example of the double empathy problem in action.

Being able to describe pain and other health experiences

in a way that people understand also links to being able to feel these things in a way that you understand and can process. This is something that many autistic people struggle with. As mentioned previously, the official name is alexithymia, which in simple terms means being unable to recognize or understand your internal states. This might be a difficulty in understanding your own emotions, or in processing your internal feelings like thirst, tiredness, or hunger. We might be able to understand how we feel, but telling someone in a way that they understand can be impossible. Sometimes we can't express, feel, or understand any of what is occurring inside of ourselves.

## Things that can help
### 'I'm autistic and that means...'
Telling healthcare professionals about being autistic can feel daunting but often it is useful for them to know. I almost wish my medical notes came with a flag waved in their face telling them to treat me with kindness because I'm autistic. A clinician offering a bit of compassion and empathy and giving someone space to orient themselves goes a long way in medical interactions.. For 'incidental' interactions where I'm seeing someone for a brief time, I don't always mention autism. That is unless I have to, or if saying 'I'm autistic, please slow down or I might not explain things in the way you expect me to' will help.

On those occasions when telling a clinician or someone in a healthcare setting is useful, I find having that having a prepared list of key things I need and feel comfortable sharing is what works best for me. I have this saved in a note on my phone. It isn't a piece of paper that can get lost. I have the option to say them to a clinician or to show them my screen if I can't get my words out. Plus, I'm never without my phone or a charger so it can't go missing.

Some people might find prompts are more useful for figuring out what to say other than 'Please check I understand you' or 'I need to be somewhere quiet'. In these cases, borrowing from hospital passports, which are used for people with a learning disability, can be useful. Some hospitals have specific versions that they use and recognize. Having the information in a format that is accessible to you is the most important part of a passport. A hospital passport asks key questions that help clinicians and healthcare staff understand how you like to be cared for, what inclusion means for you, and what your experience of health looks like. The best hospital passport I have seen was originally developed by Gloucester Partnership NHS Trust, but you can find the layout that best suits you by having a look around the internet.

Sharing your information about your access needs with healthcare staff should make things easier and mean that you are supported in accessing services. This doesn't always happen, but it should make things better, not worse. I want to emphasize that sharing your needs is something you choose to do: you choose whom you tell and what they are told. You can share as much or as little information as you want. Figuring out what works best for you to tell healthcare staff is a process. I've found keeping it short works best for me and opening the discussion with 'I'm autistic; for me that means...' helps manage some of the pre-existing stereotypes people might hold.

## Calmer sensory environments

I don't know about you, but I hate waiting rooms. It's not that I hate waiting; I just hate the sensory environment that most waiting rooms, hospitals, clinics, and medical spaces create. They're always overly loud and bright, have too much information on the wall, and the intercom systems never feel that well thought out. I'd love to be able to put on noise-cancelling headphones and shut the world out while waiting, but often that isn't feasible if patient announcements are only auditory.

Given that most places where you're a patient can make anxiety worse it would make sense for these spaces to build in calmer atmospheres. Unfortunately, most healthcare systems are too overstretched trying to provide care to think about the aesthetics, form, and function of spaces. We might not be able to ask people to dim the lights, make things less echoey, or manage the temperature, but there are things we can do to make the space fit our needs.

When having a medical appointment, whether online or in person, I always make sure I have a few objects and strategies to hand:

1. Wear noise-cancelling headphones or ear defenders or anything that you can use to take charge of what you hear. Some people use earplugs that prevent as much noise as possible; they don't block your whole ear so do let some noise in. For some the more discreet option is preferred and for others having big things that cover their ears works much better. I like how my headphones cover my ears, block sound, and help me control my environment. Sometimes headphones have the dual purpose of managing noise *and* showing others not to talk to you.

2. Have something to make notes with or ask to record the conversation. Having notes or something to listen back to can help in those times when you're unable to take anything in and need to process what happened later. Not everyone will say yes to recording, so being equipped to write things down (either on actual paper or a phone) means you're ready. You can never be over-prepared, so you may want to write down in advance the questions you want to ask and have any paperwork you might need there with you.

3. Ask for people to slow down or talk to you in a quieter space. It sounds obvious, but it isn't always apparent what might be making things harder to process or understand. You can also ask people to repeat or re-explain what they've said if it doesn't make sense. You don't have to nod as if everything is fine when it isn't.

4. Have your stim toys with you; there's no shame in what helps you regulate so make sure you've got it to hand. If I forget mine, I'm often fiddling with something anyway, whether it be a bit of fabric or something from my bag, or I might be making patterns with my fingers. Stim toys help with your need to regulate in the moment, but don't forget about the other parts of your body that also need fuelling: pack a snack and something to drink in case you get hungry or thirsty. Having something with you means you won't have to do an anxious dash to tame a grumbling stomach or a parched throat.

5. If you can or if it's appropriate have someone with you (not necessarily for one-to-one therapy) who can help you to advocate for yourself. If you do bring someone along, have a conversation with them in advance about what you want to get out of an appointment or the key things you need help with. It can also be useful to have these written down in case you forget while talking with a healthcare professional.

Through practice and reality, you find what works well for you and what isn't feasible to do; these things can change as you get older. I wasn't as able to advocate for myself when I was younger, and nor did I realize how helpful it was to have things written down to refer to when I was anxious. Your confidence in these situations can be built up by clinicians who listen to you or absolutely crushed by those who belittle you. You deserve inclusive healthcare; you deserve to be listened to, to get answers, to get support, and to get them at the right time.

## Burnout
### What is autistic burnout?

As autistic people, we can experience episodes of burnout. Smaller episodes of burnout can be the exhaustion that comes with socializing, sensory overload, or the physical exhaustion from having a meltdown or a shutdown. Bigger episodes of burnout are thanks to too much overwhelm. This could be caused by responsibility, sensory overwhelm, balancing emotions, social expectations, and everything else we must juggle. Autistic people are more likely to experience burnout because we have fewer resources to deal with these things than non-autistic people.

It is important to note that this can happen to absolutely anybody. Sometimes, trying to manage all these responsibilities can make burnout worse. When you're already exhausted and fail to complete tasks, managing them becomes even harder. Conserving your energy, not overextending yourself, and finding a way to stay on top of things means you get to preserve energy rather than barrel through to exhaustion, or so I'm told. Life doesn't always accept these boundaries; it always tries to demand more.

It's difficult to believe that you can say no, that you can do less, and that you don't have to push yourself. There are parts of life that you can let slip. You can do infrequent laundry, you can make easy meals, you can use transport that requires less planning, and you can cancel the plan that feels like too much. It doesn't feel nice to do, especially if you are a people pleaser, but it is possible and the consequences aren't world-ending, just world-pausing or -slowing.

If you experience autistic burnout you may start to notice the pattern it follows for you. There are some similarities that we all share, but it is ultimately an individual experience. Each person has their own tolerance or coping level. Everyone has their own signals of impending burnout and their own ways of recovering.

What does autistic burnout look like?
Autistic burnout differs from non-autistic burnout in how it looks or at least feels on the inside. Symptoms of autistic burnout might include:

- A loss of or reduction in your ability to use the skills you have, for example, reduced cognitive, thinking, or processing ability. You may also experience a loss of executive function skills, worsened abilities in spoken and written communication, and an inability to do what you're used to doing easily.
- Increased sensitivity to everything. This could include increased sensory sensitivity, increased emotional sensitivity, being more sensitive to change, and being more sensitive to the demands of socializing.
- An increase in autistic behaviours or appearing 'more autistic' to other people than you usually do. You may have a decreased ability to mask your autistic behaviour or feel less in control of your 'autisticness', which might present as more stimming and finding additional comfort in your special interests. Communication can be impacted through difficulties with speech, difficulties with socializing, avoiding eye contact more (if you do give eye contact usually), and struggling with empathy.
- Situations become more overwhelming more quickly. You may have more frequent meltdowns or shutdowns and these may be more physical or draining than usual.
- Chronic exhaustion that can't be remedied by resting. Sleep no longer offers relief or restoration because your brain is stuck in preservation mode and never goes into rest mode.

What might the signals or triggers look like?
I'm going to share some of my signals and triggers. You might relate to them or find that yours are completely different. Signals of burnout for me can be things like:

- losing my speech (more frequently or completely)
- frequent and escalating headaches or migraines
- being hypersensitive to my senses
- being more irritable or grumpy

- more meltdowns and shutdowns
- physical pain in my joints and increased muscle tiredness or cramps
- brain fog and processing slowness.

Changes in the routines I do to help make myself feel safe or even just my day-to-day life can push me towards burnout when combined with these triggers or signals.

Burnout is also linked to and impacted by changes to your education, starting a new year or school, assignment deadlines, changes at work, changes in friendships, increases in mental health distress, and worsening of physical health. Life is a juggling act and, unfortunately, some of these 'balls' are much more difficult to manage than others.

With non-autistic burnout someone might experience overwhelm around their work or life. There are some similarities between different types of burnout. However, they are not the same in terms of causes, experiences, and potential 'remedies' or 'treatments'. Reading about professional burnout and autistic burnout might offer you a broader understanding of what burnout means for others and how they have managed to find their way out. It can also help provide you with some of the language that other people will understand when you talk about burnout.[7]

### What can I do to prevent burnout?

It can feel like burnout is inevitable, although I hope I haven't made it seem that way from what you've read so far. Nonetheless, some things can help you to build boundaries between yourself and a potential period of burnout.

The first tip is the biggest step that I made, and it took someone else reflecting on it with me for me to be able to do

---

7   You may have guessed that I'm a big fan of the power of language and how it enables the articulation of things that can feel indescribable – until you can describe them that is. This is the same for burnout as it is many topics within autism and beyond.

it. Recognizing what your signs of burnout are and at what stage they develop are both key to changing the course from burnout to recovery. Once you know the signs you can build a prevention/recovery plan.

1. Recognize *your* signs of autistic burnout; this was the biggest thing that helped me to be able to put the proverbial brakes on and not tunnel towards deeper burnout.
2. Prioritize your 'must-do-or-else-the-world-falls-apart' tasks. Everything feels like a must, but I promise you not everything is. Having a conversation with family members, friends, employers, or educators about what you can realistically juggle is better in the long term.
3. Find time for white space in your calendar – the time that can be spent just staring at the ceiling if you need to. Even when I'm not heading towards burnout I plan for 'no thoughts, head empty' moments. They're great times to allow yourself to feel the full value of rest rather than trying to force productivity and efficiency into every waking moment.
4. Factor in time to recover, you will need it. Trust me, you need it, and you can get to a point where you have an idea of how draining something might be and how long you want to plan in recovery from it. You need recovery time and building it into your life is the best gift you can give future you.
5. Learn to *actually* say no and stick to it. I'm terrible at this! However, this is a book of advice and 'sage wisdom' based on my looking back at what I've done wrong, what I cringe at, and things I would tell my younger self to do differently. Saying no means you have more time to do the things you want rather than the things you oblige yourself to do.
6. It's okay to leave situations that overwhelm and exhaust you. We're told when we're younger that we must stick

things out, but we don't have to stay where we feel uncomfortable. You can leave, and you can allow yourself to be in spaces you enjoy being in – as long as they're safe of course!

## What can I do to get out of a period of autistic burnout or autistic fatigue?

I don't have as much good advice for this as I'd wish. I've experienced quite a few episodes of burnout, so you'd expect me to be a pro at dishing out advice on what to do. Sadly, that's not the case. The most useful advice I can offer is:

- Expectations do not equal reality. I thought I could do so much, but I found that my capacity to do things was lower than it had been. Showering took more energy than I thought and composing sentences felt like there were lead weights in my brain that stopped anything coherent from coming out. Sometimes you need to readjust your parameters to be more realistic.
- When it feels like you're coming out of burnout don't rush yourself. Progress can be celebrated too soon, which can set you back more than you'd like. It's like stopping your antibiotics as soon as you feel they're starting to work. If you don't take the full course of antibiotics, you're in danger of not making a full recovery.
- Find supportive people to be around you who will help to get you back to where you want to be. This sounds vague and I'm sorry about that! Having people who will help lift you when you struggle to lift yourself is imperative. Whether it's someone to help with chores or just someone who understands your need to go slower, you need people who will be there to support you.

## A personal experience with burnout and exhaustion

Burnout was something I didn't come to recognize until I was at university. I found myself in a five-week cycle of being okay, then completely short-circuiting for a week before needing to reboot for upcoming lectures. This system of exhaustion worked thanks to my burnout aligning with the academic calendar of 11- or 8-week terms, but it was unsustainable. I got to the point of complete destruction at which I lost my ability to verbally communicate. I had constant migraines, I became socially isolated, and I considered dropping out of university. I found all the paperwork, talked to university staff about how to leave, and planned my escape route.

I thought the pressures of university were the problem. What I didn't know at the time was that while university contributed to my burnout, it wasn't the sole reason for it. For me, the root cause was linked to the social pressures I put on myself and the masking I used when attempting to fit in.

I did recover from that devastating period of burnout over the Christmas break of my third year of university. I realized this was part of a deeper pattern of burnouts that I had experienced throughout my life. It always revolved around the same thing: I overextended myself in social situations or with my workload, not thinking about the energy that was being sucked out of me by doing more than merely existing. It was hard to realize that undertaking anything more than the bare minimum was a weight I couldn't manage. I wanted to do things! I wanted to be excited! However, what I needed to learn was how to balance and plan around my energy.

Burnout has always been a pattern of becoming so overwhelmed that parts of me just begin to shut down. My biggest triggers are always around social situations or sensory overload. What I hadn't realized was that social situations, sensory overload, and meltdowns always came with a distinct hangover or mini burnout that I couldn't explain before. No one had ever taken the time to explain to me what these feelings and experiences were, it was always seen as just part of who I was.

You might have heard burnout talked about in relation to stress, anxiety, and depression in employment. There is a much louder conversation about what burnout from your job looks like that obscures the conversation about autistic burnout. Whenever I've spoken to a clinician, they've never taken my autistic assertions about burnout seriously. This has meant I've had to slot it into frameworks they understand. I've minimized the impacts of autistic burnout by comparing it to 'work stress' so as to use language that overstretched and autism-unaware doctors will understand. We shouldn't have to make ourselves small.

I've never been able to process burnout while it was happening and that's okay – I had zero processing power to do anything at the time. It is only with distance and time that I've been able to process how complete burnout can be and how impactful even brief periods of burnout are.

# Transitions, Changes, and the Strategies for Dealing with Them

### What is a transition?

Transition is defined as a process or a period of change from one state or condition to another. Or to put it even more simply: 'to go through a change'. Life is something that can go through lots of little and big changes.

Transition is a word that gets used a lot when talking about autism and autistic young people in particular. Instead of talking about a change of school, age, or employment, it is referred to as the process of transition. What might be seen as a simple or uncomplicated thing for non-autistic people is turned into something else entirely. We face more complexity, heightened anxiety, and more external involvement. In professional speak, we don't change school we 'transition into a new provision', we don't grow up we 'transition to adulthood or adult services', we don't stop a task and start a new one, instead we have 'activity transitions'.

There are major points of 'transition' in life, but transition is something that we do every single day. Every change or choice is a transition and many of them are much smaller and more frequent than the transitions we are told to worry about. Technically, you don't ever *need* to worry about transitions but some create elevated levels of anxiety. These are the ones that might involve more planning or mean we leave something behind and move on to the next thing.

Some people can find the word transition 'othering'. It highlights that an experience which could and should be seen as normal is different to what others do. When 'transition' is used to talk about the change that autistic people experience it separates that change from something that other people are allowed to do without fanfare. This plays into the idea of disabled people just going about their business being thought of as 'inspirational'. Moving into a new house, changing school, starting a job, starting a new hobby, volunteering somewhere new, or making choices isn't inspirational – it's just life. This is part of a bigger debate and conversation that isn't for here, although I will say that the idea a disabled person is inspirational for doing something normal indicates how low people's expectations are for the disabled.

The focus on transition and inspiration never felt right to me. It feels too formal and turns what is considered an ordinary experience into something that should be viewed as extraordinary, even if it doesn't feel that way. We all have these changes, but attaching extra words and complications to them adds a layer of separation that isn't necessary.

Anyway, back on topic! Looking briefly at some of the bigger transition points in life we can see why these might be more complex for autistic people:

1.  Education. Changing your school year or school can be intimidating because it means new teachers, new classrooms, new classmates, and potentially new learning needs. If you're identified as having a 'special educational need or disability' then you might also have a plan outlining the support you need.
2.  In England, this is an Education, Health and Care plan (EHC plan) for school and college and Disabled Students Allowance (DSA) for university. There are many other legal frameworks for outlining support needs

that might be used, both nationally and internationally. Incorporating that extra step of support might mean an education move is more complex than if you didn't have support needs to access education.

3. Lining up, for example, legally mandated therapies, supports, staff, equipment, and understanding from education providers is a lot more work. The preparation and coordination for education is something other people don't have to worry about in the same way. It's far easier if you don't have needs and resources to coordinate. Many more people are involved in changes to education for disabled learners, and everything is intentionally carefully orchestrated to get things just right for you.

4. Employment. Starting a new job might be the major transition point that people typically think of for employment. However, there are also transitions and changes in every aspect of work or volunteering that you might experience. For example, deciding you want to get a job involves looking for positions, applying, interviews, and accepting offers of employment. Once you secure a job you will face a lot of smaller transitions and changes encapsulated into one big one. You'll find yourself with a new place to go to, a new route, new people, new routines, new activities, new responsibilities, new skills to learn, and new challenges. Leaving a job is also a big transition, whether you're leaving for good reasons or for upsetting reasons. It's a massive shift from what has become your routine to the thing that is potentially new, different, and not fully expected.

5. The point is, starting something is always seen as the point of transition, but when you think about how many changes there might be in employment and volunteering, there's so much more to it.

6. Getting older. For autistic people in later adolescence instead of getting ready to move out or become more independent, the transition period is often called

transition to or preparation for adulthood. Many different aspects of getting older need to be thought through, including where to live, whether to work, study, or volunteer, and changes to social rules as environments change. It can feel like others have more options and decisions that they get to make and are less constrained by what a parent, guardian, or carer allows them to decide. We continue to make these decisions alone or with the help of others throughout our lives for as long as we live. Little things are always coming up or changing as life never settles down to a fixed constant.

## Educational transitions
### Starting college, university, training courses, apprenticeships, and supportive education
This can be an intimidating transition to go through because it generally means starting something entirely new, somewhere entirely new. You never know what to expect if you haven't experienced the situation before. To try to make the move easier you can ask for an additional induction or some walkthrough sessions so that you can get to grips with orienting yourself.

It can feel overly complex to arrange an orientation if this isn't something your new education provider normally does, but it is a reasonable adjustment you can request. You might want additional help finding routes between spaces you will use frequently. It also could be useful to get to know the staff members you will interact with or at least what they look like, what their role is, and how to contact them. Finding spaces where you can relax or take breaks might also be helpful. I did an early induction at university that helped me to figure out where the quieter study spaces were, who my key contacts were, and what other support was available to me. Things like this are useful in helping future students find their footing before leaping into a new space, and many education providers routinely organize events like this now.

Having your access needs clearly communicated to your new education provider can also assist in that transition. I've found that having these written down under clear categories helps with any potential miscommunication and makes it much easier to share them. Splitting your needs into clear headings and what is needed by/shown to whom (specific teachers or support staff or classmates/peers, for example) is a useful way of doing this. For example, in communication from others I prefer explicit, verbal instructions, followed by written instructions and for things to be made specific not vague. This could be as simple as 'I need to talk to you about this assignment for this class' instead of 'I need to talk to you about something important'. For communication *with* others, I share what my communication looks or sounds like so people don't confuse what participation and chatting look like for me with me being rude or not paying attention.

### Finishing education, what now?

Finishing education and then trying to figure out what to do next can be incredibly overwhelming. Just because there is a whole world of opportunity open to you doesn't mean that choosing the opportunities you want to pursue is easy. One of the hardest things about choice that I've found is that it only gets harder when there is too much to choose from. I much prefer when things are filtered and less overwhelming.

I've finished education a couple of times and then jumped back into it again. I've tried the different pathways open to me and the different options someone might apply for or take. I finished my undergraduate degree and instead of going out into the world of employment (not for lack of trying or applying) I did a Master's degree. After that graduation, I then spent three years in employment building skills and working with autistic people. After that, I've dived back into education to study for a doctorate using the skills I had developed in employment. In the time since finishing my Master's degree I have undertaken three paid jobs, four volunteering posts, three research projects, a little bit of freelance consultancy, and then jumped back into education again while writing this book. Everyone's route is different. Evidently, I couldn't make my mind up, so tried a bit of everything. Sometimes doing a few things to find out what you want to do is exactly what is needed. When I talk about this route to other people it makes perfect sense to them, but while you're in the middle of it, exploring your options, it can feel like a maze with no clear path. Every step you take, whether big or small, continues to build towards the future you choose for yourself.

Education does end, even if I keep throwing myself into degrees. It generally ends with the award of a qualification, for example, the end-of-school qualification or a college or university degree. Moving on to the next thing generally takes extensive planning to figure out what you want to do. For this transition, I suggest talking to friends, family, mentors, or career advisors to support you in your decision-making. They might provide some insight into the paths you can take, how to plan towards your goal, and what you might need to achieve your goal.

When it comes to 'what next' you might have a clear idea or only a vague awareness of what you want to do. Having a clear idea makes this transition easier – you can work through clear steps in your plan. I didn't have a clear idea. I knew what skills I had gained through talking to career advisors and through work experience. I sort of knew what I enjoyed doing. Turning all of that into things I could do as a job and knowing the right level to apply for was a little bit difficult, but is a skill that can be learnt or taught.

## Employment transitions
### Finding a job
Figuring out where to start is a huge part of why this feels so intimidating. Breaking it down into easier-to-process aspects can make it a tiny bit easier. Turning the mountain into manageable molehills or defined steps to the top is easier than

doing everything at once. Whenever I've started looking for a job, I've broken it down into manageable tasks and reflective questions. What roles do I want to do? What sort of places or organizations do I want to work in? Whom do I want to work with? How practical or impactful do I want what I do each day to be? Does this job pay well enough to cover my rent? How many hours do I want to work?

In real terms, this means I normally have looked for jobs that have set projects or tasks, as these roles play to my strengths of working on things I know the boundaries of. That could be in a shop working as a retail assistant, working in a charity on specified projects, or designing something with people. I've worked in different sectors to figure out the areas I do and don't want to work in. Figuring out where you would be happy working and where you can't imagine yourself can help narrow down your search.

Finding a job is a balance between two things. Do you find a job you are passionate about and that is linked to your interests, or do you work somewhere that is strictly a job? If something is just a job this can make relaxation easier as your work feels unconnected to the rest of your world. If you work in areas that you are passionate about the boundary between work and not work becomes more blurred. There is a balance between a job being a 'calling' or 'dream job' and it being a way to help you pay rent, buy food, and do the things that you enjoy doing. This balance sits in how much you like a job, how much it pays you to enjoy some freedom, and the hours of freedom you have if you choose part-time or full-time work.

Once you've figured out some of these answers for yourself you can look for jobs to apply for. You can do this by following companies who advertise their roles on social media, by looking on job boards, or by talking to friends and family about roles that they know are available.[1]

---

1    There is more about employment and applying for jobs in the 'Moving on to Employment' chapter, so I haven't gone into too much depth here.

## Starting a job

Starting a job is a celebration (hurrah, you got the job!) but it is also a stressful time. You need to make sure you've shared all the right paperwork, figured out what a first day/week/month looks like, and meet new people who know each other better than you know them.

If you've chosen to share with your new workplace that you are autistic, you can ask your new manager for help with starting your new job. You may want to outline to them the things that you would like to know in advance and ask for structure around your first couple of weeks. I find explaining to them what 'thriving' looks like for you and what 'surviving' looks like can be useful to build a foundation of understanding. Planning for this transition is hopefully easy. I say 'hopefully' because it's a topic that is extensively written about as many people are nervous about starting a new job. It's never exactly easy starting something new, but with the advice of others and by learning what is important to you at the beginning of a new job, it doesn't have to be as intimidating as it might be.

Most jobs should have a gentle settling-in period. These are something you shouldn't take for granted, but they let you figure out what you're meant to be doing and how you are meant to be doing it. Take advantage of these slightly easier weeks and lowered expectations to figure out what it is you might need to support you and the things that you might find more difficult.

## Finishing a job

Finishing up and saying goodbye is never easy, but sometimes it is exactly what you need to do. You might have decided that you want a new job and so you need to leave your current job; you may need a break before working again or need to leave a workplace before looking for a new job. Sometimes you might even have a promotion, which means you're not leaving the company you work for, just the role you have been doing.

Thankfully these sorts of transitions are easier because of their clear structure. You have a notice period that you fulfil before finishing, you might have a leaving party, an exit interview, and the opportunity to prep some of your workload for whoever takes on your role after you. What can be more difficult are all the emotions around finishing a job and the emotions of change – as much as you can prepare for them they still can become overwhelming.

## Moving your life somewhere else
### Finding somewhere to live

This one is tricky whether you're moving to a new town/city or moving within a city. There is a lot of change to contend with in terms of choosing where to live, both in the broad (where to move) or specific (on a quieter road or near to easy transport links) sense. You then must figure out how to move your belongings, the cost of different housing options, and all the other little decisions.

There can be lots of small decisions that you have to make alongside the bigger decisions. Unfortunately, there isn't a handbook that outlines the process in as much explicit and clear detail as an autistic mind might want. If you do scour the internet, you can find some tips to help you. Generally, I've found that moving to a new home is easier to understand once you've been through it practically rather than trying to imagine it prospectively. Of course, that doesn't make the transition between homes easier if it's your first time doing it or your first time doing it alone.

### Packing up your things

Packing up your belongings, whether you do it room by room or by type, is not technically a transition but feels like one. It can cause huge emotional upheaval and make you think about all your belongings and their meaning to you. Having these moments is not insignificant, nor is it something to diminish, as you must rank what you cherish, what you can take with you, and what you can't.

I would recommend starting this transition and packing early to give yourself time to mull over the things you own and their meaning to you. This also allows time in case things go wrong or take longer than expected. I've run out of boxes while packing before and having more time to source more of them really helps, especially if you underestimate how much stuff you own.

## Moving your healthcare provider

This is a big one! I'll admit I have moved house a fair amount over a period of eight years and still haven't registered at a new doctor or dentist. It just feels too scary because I don't know what could go wrong. It's a big change to commit to, and I've not had a 'quiet part' of my healthcare journey that has allowed for this massive shift and upheaval.

I'm not great at offering advice on this as it's something that I've struggled with. I find there are too many forms and too much bureaucracy, but I know other people tackle it without this level of difficulty. It does feel comfortable sticking with what is known, especially if you have a doctor or dentist who doesn't make accessing healthcare an anxiety-ridden experience.

## Finding new routines

Something that helped me when I moved to new places was finding new things to build into my routines: finding new supermarkets and routes around them, new parks to walk around, figuring out the bus routes, finding the shops and coffee shops I wanted to sit in in the local town, and generally just finding my space. These practical things can help ground you and can also carry over from what you liked to do where you lived previously.

Not all aspects of transitions are bad, sometimes you need to focus on the good parts and the things that don't change when there is so much change happening.

# Friendships and Relationships while Autistic

Relationships are something we are told everyone wants to or should have, whether with family and friends, or a boyfriend, girlfriend, or partner. We can struggle in relationships, both in establishing them in the first place and in keeping them going. It isn't a fault or something wrong with us, just something we might find difficult. I know it's something I've found difficult at various stages of my life. A relationship isn't one-sided: both people contribute to make it the best it can be. Normal relationships and friendships will have easier times and more difficult patches, but these can be worked through. When relationships succeed or break down it can happen because of the actions of one or both people. Sometimes the influence that time and change have on relationships is too powerful for us to overcome.

## Autism and socializing

Socializing is one of those things we're told we're bad at. It's in the checklist for our diagnosis and we have to be clinically bad at talking to and relating to others to get a diagnosis. We might be worse or different to others in how we understand social rules, but that doesn't mean that we can't or won't socialize. We just prefer to do it on our own terms. That isn't something for others to look down on.

You will find ways in which to make friends, socialize, and maintain friendships or romantic relationships that work for you. Your relationships don't have to look like the idealized versions in films or on TV. We can make friends, and we can be in relationships. In fact, we can do all these things at our own pace and in our own ways. As a teenager who was severely bullied, who had boys pretend to ask me out as a joke, and who moved through friendships that often felt tumultuous, I know just how patronizing this might sound. 'It gets better' sounds like a platitude when you're in a dark moment and unable to see any positives, but it is true. We shouldn't have to go through harder times or bullying or relationships that hurt us to find people who don't do that. Unfortunately, so many of us do.

As someone on the other side of things, past all the school drama and safely surrounded by a strong support network of friends, family, and a fiancé, I can now look back and see bad things shouldn't have happened. I now have a pretty good, if small, group of people to rely on who can also rely on me. When building that circle of support and friends it was important to me that they knew I am autistic, and what that means for me. It was also vitally important that the relationships were built on the things we like about each other rather than the things we hate about others. Curating your relationships – whom they're with and how they happen – is a lesson we all learn through what works best for us. I've had experience with social skills courses, not necessarily positive, so my main advice is to find people you like who don't put too much pressure on things and just be yourself. It's far better than trying to be some false neurotypical version of you.

## Building relationships

We are told that school is the best time of our lives. It might be for some people but for others, it really isn't. Some of us don't have the good times to look back on with fond nostalgia. It's a time when friendships can flourish, and people can explore what they enjoy in life and can find common interests with others. School is this sort of 'protected space' where you can begin to figure yourself out.

This 'best time of your life' might be because it is theoretically easier to build a friendship with someone else when you spend nearly eight hours a day and five days a week with them. Some people form lots of friendships in school because of this environment. For others, this extended amount of time around their peers is not always positive. It can lead to increased bullying and short-lived friendships because there are so many more unknown rules to friendship than just liking the same thing.

The way we build friendships changes over the course of our lives. This is primarily because the environments we're in and the opportunities we have change as we get older. It is generally easier to make friends while at school because you're together for so much of your time. As you get older it can get harder to form friendships as we don't spend as much time with others in the same way. Social spaces as adults revolve around workplaces, our leisure time, our online spaces, and often spaces with alcohol.

Something that can help with building relationships, which might sound silly, is truly just being yourself. It's doing the things you like, finding people who share a similar ethos or similar views to your own, and fostering conversations with them. It is so much better for you to be authentically yourself in friendships or relationships. You build the foundation of truth into who you are with others and that is far easier to maintain than a façade of falsehoods and what you think others want.

Friendships and relationships can get off to rocky starts, or you can meet people you click with. There's no right way to befriend someone. It is a learning process of finding people you want to be friends with or in a relationship with, building a shared connection, and maintaining a reciprocal relationship.

## Maintaining relationships

Making friends can be difficult because there is no guidebook, at least none that I've found on how to make a friend or about staying friends with someone. It all depends on each interaction you have after becoming friends. However, it can be easier to keep friendships when you become friends with someone who has similar interests to you. Shared interests always help provide a topic of conversation or shared activities. Also, being at a similar stage of life to someone or them sharing the same values as you can strengthen friendships.

Staying friends with someone isn't about talking to them loads or overwhelming them with your presence – it's about sharing space in your life together. There's no set way to do that, simply because everyone has unique and individual lives. There are some friends I talk to every day, some I catch up with on no set schedule, and others I see a couple of times a year. Friendships and relationships are different for different parts of your life and that is fine. You can't judge reality according to the expectations you hold.[1]

In maintaining a friendship, you can focus on the activities that you do together, the ways that you care about someone else's life, and the value that they bring to yours. This could involve meeting up for coffee (or any other drink that you prefer) with someone, spending time discussing the things that are going on in your life, and talking about the positives and the things that you're struggling with. We often reach out to our friends for advice if we're unable to get it from family members. In many ways, friends become our chosen family. There are some things you want to talk to friends about, some things you want to talk to a romantic partner about, and some things that are for family. Building and maintaining relationships across

---

1   This isn't meant to come across as patronizing or profound – I guess I'm trying to say that once I learnt that judging relationships by how they were perceived on the outside did nothing to support my relationships, I stopped. It's so much better to do things in ways that work for you rather than ways that look 'right'.

these groups will provide you with a support system that you can lean on, and equally there will be times when those people may need to lean on you.

Practically speaking, going for coffee with someone might not be the most successful way for an autistic person to keep a friendship going because coffee shops are incredibly sensorily overwhelming. Instead, it could be that you are friends with someone and talk to them over text-based communication or through playing games together. You don't have to be physically with someone to be their friend.

Friendships rarely go easily or smoothly all the time because everyone grows and changes as they get older, and their reactions to situations evolve. It's okay to talk about the things that you value and the things that you find important in your life with someone to figure out if they feel the same. You might talk to your friends, for example, about how they view different disabilities or their views on LGBT+ rights or race or religion. Although these topics are difficult to talk about, they are important to discuss with your friends. You want to know your friends share the same views as you. As these aren't easy conversations, they might sometimes cause fights, but fights are likely to happen in any sort of relationship where you challenge each other. Having these tough discussions is one of the better reasons to fight with friends, especially if their views on human rights turn out to be suspect.

Friendships can be different when you're at school or a young adult. Rather than being the best days of your life, these are the days when people start to figure out their identity or pick on others who may not be sure of their identity. If you're not quite sure of yourself that seems to be something that bullies enjoy exploiting, even if they're insecure themselves. If you don't fit into their narrow view of what is acceptable or normal you may become a target, and they will use the thing that you stand out for to try to make you feel weaker. Being different doesn't mean you are weaker.

## When relationships aren't quite right

Sharing the same space with someone and talking to them doesn't necessarily mean they are your friend, which can be confusing. I've had instances where I thought I was friends with someone because we spent time together and did things together, but sometimes that isn't the case. It can feel embarrassing when the façade cracks and the reality becomes clear.

Some people will happily take advantage of the social struggles that autistic people have. They see us as vulnerable and easy to manipulate. Those people will say one thing to our face that sounds positive and say negative things about us to others. These are the type of people who like to surround themselves with those they view as lesser to make themselves feel better. Situations like these are called mate crime, victimization, or interpersonal victimization. People like this are not your friends no matter how much they may bring some sense of friendship into your life.

Researchers have worked with autistic people to try to understand these sorts of situations and why they happen. Dr Amy Pearson has conducted some research to help us understand this concept a bit more.[2] In some cases autistic people may find that others take advantage of their good nature – they want to please others and they also struggle to perceive when these situations happen. Often when others take advantage of us and victimize us in these ways, we might not be able to see it. We might not understand it at the time but, with hindsight, we can recognize ill intent in others.

You might recognize when you're in a relationship or friendship that you don't want to be in. You can see this by analysing how being with that person makes you feel, the way they act around you, or how others react to them. If something feels off or you begin to feel more negative than positive about

---

2   Pearson, A., Rees, J., & Forster, S. (2022). 'This was just how this friendship worked': experiences of interpersonal victimization among autistic adults. *Autism in Adulthood*, *4*(2), 141–150. https://doi.org/10.1089/aut.2021.0035

the relationship, you can end it. It won't necessarily be easy to build that distance and separation between yourself and the person or group you want to split from, but it is possible. These things hurt as you do them, but that pain reduces with time as you build positivity into your life and relationships.

For example, if it is someone you must see or interact with every day, I've found the easiest and gentlest way is to explain the things that have caused this decision. Tell them that you've decided to re-evaluate and change what influences, ideas, or actions you want in your life. It still isn't an easy thing to do, but having a way to begin those conversations about endings can be helpful. Alternatives could be not explaining why you're cutting someone off. You could ghost friends or romantic interests, but that often leaves people without closure or answers – most people want both of those things.

If it is someone you see less often or interact with through digital means, creating that separation can be easier. You can create boundaries around what you will interact with or reply to, or reduce how much digital access they have to you by muting or blocking them. The important thing to remember in any of these situations is that you have a choice in who you want to spend your time with (and others have the same choice). If something feels bad to you then you can remove that part of your life. Pruning friendships is something we all must do at points in our life, but don't prune all friendships away leaving yourself completely isolated.

## When friendships and relationships end

This one is a toughie. Everyone reacts differently when relationships end, whether they end abruptly, with a bang, or just fizzle out. It's a huge shift and change when relationships with others end. Untangling our lives from others and realizing just how intertwined they have become is one of the harder parts. If you live with someone, if they have some of your belongings, or if you have shared routines or shared interests it can make things more difficult.

These times can be filled with tension, big emotions, huge decisions, and lots of upheaval. There is no way to deal with it other than just going through it, unfortunately. You can't hide away from dealing with it or processing what has happened, you can't skip the weird admin that can come from relationships ending, and nor can you pretend it isn't happening.

I don't have as much useful advice as I'd like here. I've been hurt by friendships ending before, and I've bumbled my way through as best as I can. The easier ones are the friendships where people almost float out of your life by mutual agreement. Friends like these are ones you can always reconnect with later if you want to, but sometimes life is too busy to hold everyone in your life all the time. Friendships that end in arguments and fury are harder. The emotions can burn hot, making you guarded and unsure of yourself. In those situations, having time to protect yourself and figure things out is good to help you get back to yourself and hopefully not get into the same situation again.

What I can offer are the assurances that you deserve to be in friendships and relationships that cherish you, celebrate you, and make you feel good about yourself. Leaving ones that don't or ones that have just run their course is okay, and the hurt that follows them is something we can't avoid navigating.

# Home Life

Home life can be complex when you're autistic. Many options are open to you, but you might not have been made aware of all of them. For example, some people choose to live with their family, some choose to live alone, some live with friends or romantic partners, and some may live in supported accommodation. Home life can cause turbulence for anyone. If you spend an extended period of time with someone, they might get on your nerves a bit. However, they might also know exactly what you need for support and all the little things that you like. Generally, the positives and negatives should balance out, but the scales can tip in either direction.

A lot of these decisions are made for you when you are younger, typically by parents, guardians, carers, or whoever you live with. When you become a teenager, young person, or young adult you start to make some of these decisions by yourself. It can feel overwhelming because suddenly you're viewed as an adult. As an adult, you've got to pay bills, pay rent, magically know what needs cleaning, and when to do all these things.

Other people just seem to manage these things well. They have effective executive functioning or have been walked through these things growing up. It can feel scary and new to manage these tasks, but that's just because you've got to figure out how to do it yourself, or with the help of someone else. Once it is no longer new it becomes something we're used to, and it becomes part of our routine.

While it's not necessarily life or death where you live or

how you live, I'm not here to dismiss those anxieties. It's a daunting prospect that can be mixed with the stress of money, location, relationships, personal safety, mental wellbeing, and your physical health. Home is where we spend most of our time. The pandemic taught us all that home is a space where we work, study, socialize, cook, clean, and live. As well as being all these different multifunctional spaces home also must be somewhere we can relax, somewhere that is our own that we feel safe in. Sometimes home can shift between being negative or positive based on the relationship we have with the physical space and those that inhabit it.

Building (not always but sometimes literally) a space that can provide you refuge is important. It starts with the location you choose, whom you choose to live with, and your current requirements for a home. Building your space continues with all the little decisions about how you furnish a home or the routines you have. What you choose is up to you; you get to express your personal style as much as the space allows and figure out how to make the space somewhere that you feel comfortable. For some people, it is important to configure the visual organization of a space so it isn't visually overwhelming, and for others, it is necessary to manage the sound, lights, smells, and textures in their home environment. I've found you're either an overhead, bright light user or a lamp lover, for example. Some people don't like furniture to clutter a space and others like plenty of flat surfaces to display everything on. There are so many ways to make a space work for you and those that you live with.

You don't have to have all the answers when you start making decisions and you might make some wrong ones, but they are *your* choices for *your* life. For example, would I choose to live on a main road next to a train track in a house with no sound insulation again? No, probably not, but I now know that and can choose quieter spaces with more greenery, good transport links (not attached to the house), and amenities I can easily walk to because I have learnt that I like those things.

## Being supported by those you live with

Everyone has different access needs, preferences, and structures for how they like to live. As every person is an individual whether they are autistic or not, disabled or not, the best thing to do is to ask each person about what they need for support or what their likes and their dislikes are. This means that for those who have support needs these can be heard or acted upon, and a dialogue is opened for others who might not be as sure about what they need.

### Finding the right housemates for you

It can be useful to think about what you want or need from the physical space you want to live in and from the people you want to (or already do) live with as a first step to figuring out how you can be best supported. For example, this could be designated quiet spaces or quiet times, living with people who like to spend more time alone, or more time being with others (it doesn't have to be talking – it can be the companionable silence of doing things near someone else). You might prefer people who share the same hobbies or interests or to live close to things that are important to you. Everyone varies in what they want to do with their work or free time, how much they want to socialize online or in person, and what a place to rest and recharge looks like to them. Knowing what you want and what meets your needs is an important step in being able to tell others what these needs are. It's difficult to express what you don't know yet, so there could be some trial and error to it. Don't worry, that's normal.

There are so many ways to live with people, or not live with people if that's your preference. You might live with a romantic partner, you might live with friends, or you might live with strangers (who can become friends or enemies depending on how it goes). You might live with people who go to the same university or college as you, you might live with people who work in the same geographical area as you, and you might live close to or far away from your family. Figuring out who to live with and where to live is a personal journey based on your circumstances, whom you choose to live with, and any constraints like budget, location, and accommodation size.

I've lived with family, friends made while at university, my boyfriend/fiancé/husband, and in university halls with about 180 other students. In practical terms that has meant living with a whole mix of people. The entire process has meant I know exactly the type of person I enjoy living with and what roles I fulfil in a household; this isn't something I knew before trying out these scenarios. It comes down to a few key points:

- I like to like the people I live with; I prefer to live with people who I don't hate and who don't hold wildly opposing views to me (basically I don't like racists, homophobes, ableists, and anyone who hates other people based on their circumstances). Sounds simple, but it was a learning process to work out what I was willing to tolerate.
- I like to live with relatively clean people who help clean. I'm not a messy person; I like to live and work in clean spaces, and I think the responsibility of keeping places clean rests on everyone using them.
- I like living with people who understand my humour and share some interests with me. I'm quite a witty person, and my dry humour reflects that. I like being able to joke around and relax with people and just chat about serious or not-so-serious topics.
- I don't need to spend every minute with the people I live with – we live our own lives. However, it is nice to do things near other people: a good bit of companionable silence is amazing. Sometimes I need to rest and recharge alone and that's perfectly okay; sometimes I want to spend time with people and at other times I want to potter about doing my own thing.
- I don't like overly loud spaces and I like to live near some greenery; walking helps me to process things and

it's nicer to do in green spaces than feel like you're walking outside someone's house. In terms of practicality this means living near a park or with access to green spaces, not too near a main road as road noise can cause a constant brain hum of sensory overwhelm, and living somewhere that is well insulated so I don't hear too much from the road or neighbours.

You might be different, but these are just some points to get you thinking! Preferences come in all shapes and sizes, or more accurately, in all different areas and strengths.

## Living with different people

Depending on where you are in your life your living situation may vary. You might be at school so living with family, or you might be at university and potentially living with strangers or friends that you have made. You might be working so living with friends or someone you're in a romantic relationship with, or living your life differently to these potential scenarios.

These different phases of life might mean living in slightly different locations, mainly because of your financial means, your relationships, or your age. Previously, there would have been a lot of rigidity about what you did when, and where you lived at what age, but we're beginning to move past those stereotypes. You might stay with your parents for longer if you want to save money to buy a place of your own, or you might move out as soon as possible to rent your own space. You might also choose to live alone; all options are open to you.

### Living with family

This can be a tricky one. Some people get along with their family incredibly well, and others don't. It's not necessarily anyone's fault – sometimes personalities clash. You don't have to get along with or be palatable to every single person in the world, and they don't need to be liked by you either. We're told that we must love our family. Sometimes you can love someone without liking them all the time.

Living with family as you get older can be an awkward transition. You move from a lack of autonomy that your family have been used to when you're a child or teenager to an adult who can and does make choices about their own life. This is where I've found living with family differs from living with friends. When your parents and siblings (plus whoever else lives at home) are used to or know what you were like when you were younger, they can, often unintentionally, treat you like the previous version of yourself.

The good thing about family is that they usually know exactly what makes you happy and what makes you sad. The bad thing is they might not always get these the right way around. They know the things that can upset you, and that can mean families clash with us more than friends. Ultimately, it is your choice whether you live with family and whether that works for you or how it will work for you. What you need to remember is that family is one of the strongest constants in life. No family is perfect; sometimes relationships can work better from a distance rather than all under the same roof! I've found as an adult that not living with family has helped me create autism-friendly spaces at home more easily and has made my relationships with my family members so much better. Living with fewer people in a space I've made my own has dramatically reduced the meltdowns I've had and the amount of overload I was experiencing.

## Living with friends

It can make it a lot easier to maintain friendships when you live with your friends, but it can also put a lot more strain on these relationships. Some people are great friends but are terrible at keeping things clean. Many people are wonderful to talk to but make an absolute mess of any room or don't know how to do chores they haven't been taught. Sitcoms and shows often romanticize these sorts of living relationships or at least set them up as constant fun. While living with friends can be fun, there can also be tough conversations when things aren't working as well as they should.

Living with your friends can make planning activities together a lot easier and is one of the things that we miss as we grow older. Retrospectively, moving geographically further and further away from our friends is tough. Friends being five steps down a hallway is far better than a 50-minute drive! However, those short distances can make it harder to get the alone time that you might want and need. This will be easier if you can find a way to say 'I just want to be alone' that no one is offended by.

## Living with someone you're in a relationship with

This one is a big step in a relationship – a sign of commitment to the person you're with. You're tying yourself into a lease and finding out more about a person by living with them. Like living with friends or family, you're choosing to live with someone who can support you. They'll know (or learn) the big and little things about you, and you might find out things about them that you don't like in a housemate.

Moving in with someone you're in a relationship with is a big commitment; it can make things more difficult if you break up, but it can make your relationship stronger. Living together means combining and building routines together – something that can be a source of relief and apprehension when you're autistic. Examples include the meals you cook together, the chores that keep a house running, the way you share your weekends, spending evenings together, and creating memories together that strengthen your relationship.

## Getting others to understand autism

Some people can have misconceptions about autism: what autism is, how to support autistic people, and what to do in stressful situations. To help them it is important to consider:

- how you want your identity to be referred to: autistic person or person with autism
- how to talk about autism: you might struggle with things, but you aren't a sufferer
- getting people to think about the meaning of the language they are using: avoiding stigmatizing language in favour of more positive options.

For many autistic people, getting the language right about us is a big step in creating an inclusive and supportive environment. A step is just a start, though, and isn't the only part of being understood as an autistic person by those you live with.

As autistic people, we can face difficulties and differences in a few main areas. Each autistic person is impacted differently by our areas of autistic difference. There is a wide range of triggers for distress or frustration for autistic people and for others who struggle with mental health, trauma, and disabilities.

Top tips for figuring out what support you might need from your housemates or the people you live with are:

1. Talk to the person about what you want for support. It sounds simple, but it often isn't. Telling them you are autistic is one thing, but explaining what that means for you is another. It's always better to explain what you want or need so that they don't make assumptions on your behalf that might be wrong or detrimental.
2. Everyone wants to be included in or invited to events. Sometimes you might say no, sometimes you'll say yes to an activity, but you don't get the chance if you're not even invited! I always let people know about fluctuating energy levels and that I like being asked even if I'm not always a firm yes.
3. Emphasize that people communicate differently, and we should be equally respected whether we are highly verbal, don't use a lot of words, or communicate through

apps. This is specific to you and your communication style and needs.

4. People have different strengths and weaknesses; we should maximize people's strengths and support them in the areas they struggle with. Some people don't like phoning utility companies while others are good at getting quick help and saving money on the phone. You might not be the 'makes phone calls' housemate but you might have other strengths. It's all also about communicating and recognizing who is best at what.

5. Talk about your sensory sensitivities, whether bright lights, noise, strong smells, or anything else. It can be useful to chat these through to help reduce arguments and confrontations before they happen.

## Finding somewhere that you want to live

Finding a place to live can be difficult because there are so many things to think about:

- Where am I going to live? Can I live close to where I work/study? Or close to my friends, my family, my interests, and in an area that fits my needs exactly?
- Do I want to live in a house, a flat, by myself, with people I do know well, people I know sort of well, or absolute strangers?
- How do I find somewhere to live that is safe and legitimate?
- How much do I need to budget for rent, bills, food, activities, and saving?
- How do I know the people I might be living with are the right people for me to live with?
- How do I navigate all the legal bits of moving?
- Why is moving so hard? Why do I own so many small things that relate to my interests?

Finding a home can be more difficult when you're autistic as you may have additional needs or concerns around where you live. Having these additional concerns isn't a bad thing: you just might have more things on your checklist or wants list for somewhere to live to make sure it is somewhere you feel safe and happy.

Some top tips for flat- or house-hunting with or without housemates include:

- It's okay to be friends with someone but not want to live with them because you are complete opposites. When tidy people live with messy people or late-night socializers live with those who like to get to bed early it can lead to conflict. Save your friendship by keeping their annoying habits away from your home environment.
- Think about the practical aspects. Supermarkets, transport, bills, green spaces, busy roads, how long your commute will be, and amenities are as important as the space you live in.
- Check out the place if you can. Even though properties go quickly you never know if that weird, angled picture by the estate agent was hiding something. There could be mould, a lack of heating, dodgy floorboards, a broken kitchen, or a giant flood in the bathroom. Some people think one picture is enough, but realistically you're giving up a huge portion of your income to live somewhere, so it's better if you like it.
- Be reasonable about what you can afford. There is no point spending all your money on a nice room, if you then can't afford to enjoy yourself or pay your bills. There is also no point living far away from everything you need to get to just because it is cheaper. Balancing rent, transport costs, bills, food, saving, and activities is tricky to get right.

The main extras to think about are the sensory environment in and around where you want to live, who you are going to live with, and the structural supports you may want in the place you live, for example, cleaning rotas to save arguments, quiet time to allow winding down, or just letting people know plans in advance.

## When arguments and disputes happen

Living with others or just spending a lot of time with someone means you become more aware of the things they do well and, unfortunately, the things they do that annoy you. It could be how or when they do their washing up, the things they do to relax being too loud (or not what you consider relaxing), or perhaps they do or say something that niggles you to your core. Spending a lot of time with someone, as you tend to do when living with them, means that there is an increased chance of finding something to fight about. These things don't have to be big, and they can blow up into bigger arguments than you might think.

Most people argue at least once in the time that they know a person. Whether that person is family, a close friend, a housemate, or someone with opposing views to your own. It's likely that you will, at some point, get frustrated at, annoyed by, grumble about, and argue with a flatmate or housemate. Some disputes and arguments can be settled before they even start; others can only be sorted while they are happening and the relationship may need to be repaired after the issues have all been aired. This isn't something that will always be easy for autistic people as there are basic differences in how we process information and the world around us.

Often, people rely on body language, inference, or 'what is unsaid'. However, if something isn't explicit then not everyone will be able to pick up on the meaning that is meant to be there. That makes sense to me as an autistic person as something that should be understood. Unfortunately, we can often be seen as quite blunt or direct in our communication; we don't utilize all the nuances that non-autistic people do. We might not use non-verbal communication in the same way as them or understand what they are sharing with theirs. This trait and a no-nonsense approach to communication can appear quite harsh, especially during an argument when everyone is more sensitive, especially to the nuances of communication.

Here are some tips for solving and avoiding disputes with those you live with:

- Set clear rules, be explicit about your expectations, and talk about the things that all of you like or dislike. That way everyone knows what is expected of them. Reading between the lines isn't something everyone can do. Figuring out hidden meaning is something you might be able to do with someone you have known for a long time, but knowing exactly what they mean isn't always guaranteed.
- Comments about someone else's hygiene or habits should never be personal. Someone's personal hygiene, habits, or ways of doing things are normally things that they have learnt and applied throughout their whole life so can't be changed instantly – that's why they're habits. Instead, think about how to talk about the way they do something and the way that you do something. You might be able to reach a compromise. Approaching these things can be tricky as their behaviour might be the result of insecurity or a sign of their health worsening.
- Communicate as well and as kindly as you can. No one reacts well to being told off through passive-aggressive Post-it notes or not-so-passive-aggressive shouting. It just doesn't work, and nor do highly anxiety-provoking showdowns where there is a huge amount of criticism levelled at just one person. When little disagreements start to escalate to arguments you need to remember

that you will be living with that person before, during, and after the disagreement. Settling disagreements in a way that meets everyone's needs is necessary, at least to some extent. This doesn't mean you have to let someone else win every argument. Everyone needs to compromise at some point, and compromise isn't always equal or 50/50.

- When you talk about something don't make people feel like they can't escape. An open and honest conversation that someone can start, stop, and finish later in ways that work for them is often better. Having a conversation when emotions are high and there is every chance of someone saying something they regret can be a bad idea, and it's usually better to revisit the conversation when everyone has had a chance to calm down.

I've always found it is often easy for grumbles and smaller disputes to turn into housemates not talking to each other. If you're annoyed at someone you might not want to even speak to them (we have all probably experienced 'the silent treatment' at some point). This can be good because you then don't say any unkind things, but it also can completely stall communication and any chance of solving disputes. The most important thing to remember is that disputes will invariably happen. Nothing is okay 100 per cent of the time – that just isn't how the world works. You can't control whether a confrontation happens, but you can control your reactions and actions.

# Society

As I take a social model approach to disability it makes sense that I've got a lot of ideas concerning how society can change to best support autistic and (otherwise) disabled people. There have been dramatic shifts in how autism is conceptualized and understood by wider society. How we now understand what autism is and what an autistic person looks like[1] is incredibly different to how things used to be.

Additionally, there have been many changes in the supports available to us as disabled people in public spaces, and in the perceptions of us – both in the media and the general public – over the course of autistic history. Some of this is due to changes in legislation towards inclusive or accessible practice, changes in how we are managed (the deinstitutionalization movement), and the broadening understanding of what autism is. Thankfully, this has filtered down into society and is not just in the heads of those interested in autism. It is great that change is happening but that doesn't mean this cultural shift has happened at a universal rate. Even comparing the early 2010s to where we are now, autism is a much more prominent feature of societal consciousness with more programmes, portrayals, news stories, and just stuff about autism. It might not all be perfect or positive, but people are much more aware of autism and autistic people than they used to be.

---

1    Autism doesn't have a specific look necessarily; you can't guess whether someone is autistic just by looking at them but the idea of what an autistic person 'looks like' in terms of stereotypes has diversified hugely and rightfully throughout history.

There is a lot of work involved in shifting public perception and understanding in both individual and collective senses. It is difficult to measure the success of public awareness campaigns and assess whether tangible differences have been made. Some people know what autism is and support autistic people well. Unfortunately, others may not: they may struggle to explain or define what autism is but can vaguely recognize the word autism. Although there is a reasonable, broad level of understanding about autism in the general public, this hasn't advanced in all areas equally. Some of the public perception is still rooted in myths and stereotypes about autism and, for some, autism is still a condition that holds stigma or invites fear. We have some allies out there, but not everyone supports autistic people in the best ways.

## Community
### Creating our own community

Like any group that has shared characteristics or a shared understanding, autistic people can come together to form the autistic community. Community doesn't have to be a physical place, but it can be. Community can be a discord server, friends you make online, companionship you find with similar people, fighting for our collective rights, and supporting other autistic people to solve problems. Autistic culture is important. It encapsulates the things that define us as a collective autistic community, and it is filled with the things we do and create. Although our community and culture may not have existed for centuries like other groups and identities, we as autistic people have developed a community and culture together. We've done this partially because of the need for advocacy for our community and partially to celebrate our unique contributions to the world.

We haven't always had an autistic community – sometimes it has been fractured and difficult to reach. Sadly, people don't always understand the importance or existence of the autistic community. Due to stereotypes about autistic people being lonely, isolated, antisocial, or otherwise lacking interest in others, people might assume that we don't want to be a part of a community. They're wrong! Whether you know it or not, whether you seek it out or not, you are and will always be a welcome part of the autistic community. There will always be someone on the other side who will understand you, your autistic self, and what you are going through.

## The importance of community

The autistic community is always there; its presence is as important as it is political. For me, the autistic community was something I first found while on the waiting list for a diagnosis. I began to explore #ActuallyAutistic on Tumblr (it was 2012–2014 so it was a different time on the internet). It was something I stumbled upon accidentally while trying to figure out who I was. Fortunately, I found myself looking at posts that I resonated with. For the first time, I was reading explanations and watching videos that I could fully relate to. Finding so much similarity, when I had been told for so long that I was weird and unlike so many other people, shook the very foundations of what I thought about myself. It was quite disorientating and new – a new feeling of being like someone else. I wasn't broken – I just hadn't seen myself or people like me represented positively before.

You are not broken; we are not broken; a society that tells us we are broken beyond repair is the most broken part of all of this. I realized I was never broken; I was just made to feel that way for so long because the world refused to handle me feeling better about myself. So often the conceptualization of autism is not of autistic people thriving but of autistic trauma and distress. When we are allowed to define ourselves and create our community, we can reframe this away from trauma and towards success or even neutrality.

What I really learnt from the community I discovered was the strength that you can find in a community connected by similarity. I found my community on Tumblr, on Twitter, by meeting other disabled people, by working at disability- and autism-focused charities, and by listening to so many people. We don't always have to base our entire connection on autism, but it's the path that leads us to a similar place so that we can find so many other things to connect through.

That's the real importance of our community: it's the shared understanding, the mutual admiration, knowing that everything will be okay and that nothing needs to be hidden. We can and should have pride in being autistic: it is not something that is wrong with us, it *is* us. There can be challenges, there can be moments we hate – the consequences of how others perceive us or how the world hurts us – but we can always return to the support and encouragement of our community.

That's not to say that any community is a perfect space in which everyone gets along – that just isn't realistic. Someone being autistic doesn't mean you will automatically get along. What it does mean is that you might have some shared place of understanding to start from. When engaging with the autistic community online it's likely that you will find people with similar experiences or opinions to yours, but you might not. You don't have to dive in all the way – you can figure out how you want to interact with the community. The autistic community, at least in online spaces, is like any group: there are cliques to some extent, people are often guarded (especially if they've been hurt in the past), and many just want to help other autistic people.

The autistic community, both online and in person, can be a great place for support and learning from others but can feel incredibly overwhelming at times. Everyone is at different points on their journey of learning about autism, the politics that surround us, and the language that describes us, which can make interacting with people feel incredibly high stakes – especially if you (like me) worry about offending people. So, tread gently and do what is right for you.

## Sexuality

Autistic people shouldn't be desexualized just for being autistic, but we often are. Many people want romantic and sexual relationships with others. We've moved on from shows like *The Undateables* to *Love on the Spectrum*, which is a small shift from 'This person isn't someone I could date' to 'Look, *those* people are okay to date'. It isn't necessarily better, and it is a smaller step than I'd like.

Autistic relationships and experiences of sexuality might not fit neatly with the heteronormative views of what relationships might look like. Our struggles with social relationships can spill over into romantic relationships. Regardless of social struggles, the person you choose to be in a relationship with should respect and celebrate you rather than make you feel uncomfortable. As I said, autistic relationships might not be heteronormative and you might have different romantic or sexual preferences to the normative idea of relationships with someone of the 'opposite gender'. In fact, autistic people are more likely than non-autistic people not to be heterosexual. We're much more likely to have different sexual attractions or to want to experience romantic relationships in a different way than non-autistic people.

Your romantic interests and sexuality are two separate, but connected things.[2] An example of this might be if someone is asexual but is bi-romantic. They might not have a high desire for or 'interest' in sex but enjoy romantic relationships with people of genders like and different to their own. Your sexuality and romantic interests may align, or they may diverge; they can change over time as you come to understand yourself better. It doesn't mean that the labels you have for yourself

---

.2    If you want to learn about more sexuality in relation to autistic people, Erin Ekins has written an incredibly comprehensive book on the subject. *Queerly Autistic* is a one-stop shop for answering questions you might have, offering reassurance and a place of safety in being who you are.

earlier in life were wrong – they were just as right as you could express at the time.

Sexuality can come with the same difficulties around disclosure as you might experience when talking about being autistic. You can and should have pride in all your identities whether that is being autistic, bisexual, lesbian, or aromantic.

## Ableism

Ableism is a type of discrimination that disabled people face. Ableism is experienced by autistic people, but these experiences might be different or not as obvious as the ableist experiences of other disabled people.

Discrimination is broadly described as when a person is treated badly by another person because of aspects of their identity. Often discrimination is based on what people perceive, see, or think about others whom they judge as lesser than themselves, which results in them treating the other person poorly. Some types of discrimination are conscious, others subconscious. They might be done maliciously or with the intent to hurt others, or they might not be. A person may not realize that their actions, words, and thoughts are harmful to others if they have not been challenged for these views and actions previously. Then again, they might know exactly what they're doing.

The most important thing is that your feelings about how someone acts towards you, whether they intend to harm you or not, are completely valid. What someone might think of as a joke or not harmful can be harmful to you. Instances of ableism can sometimes be hard to spot as they can be frequent occurrences. These instances can be small and quick or bigger and harder to ignore. Depending on how you're feeling you may brush them off or challenge them.

Ableism might be actions that a non-disabled person does, something that a disabled person does to another disabled person, or something that you might do to yourself (this is called internalized ableism). Anyone can be ableist in their actions and words. It is through learning what hurts others that people become actively anti-ableist by removing slurs from their vocabulary, acting in inclusive ways, and supporting others rather than harming them.

Ableism actions might be exclusionary behaviours like not listening to or acting upon disabled people's access needs, or presuming incapability and doing things for disabled people when they are fully capable of doing them themselves. Another example is saying people are inspirational for doing things simply because they are disabled. Using language to be ableist might include ableist slurs like 'idiot', 'retard', 'cripple', or 'crazy'.

Ableist people exclude and discriminate against disabled people in big and small ways. They don't accept our differences and think we're making our needs up. They refuse to make environments accessible for us and ensure that we can't share the same spaces as them (education providers, neighbourhoods, jobs, and public spaces). Some obvious signs of ableism are abuse or bullying that directly relates to being disabled.

Ableism impacts all disabled people and has different impacts and outcomes for those with different disabilities. A wheelchair user might face ableism through the lack of lifts, ramps, or wide-enough doorways, or by being referred to as 'wheelchair bound', which forgets the enabling part of a wheelchair as an access aid. A Deaf person might face ableism (or specifically audism) through not having access to sign interpretation or captions, and people saying 'Don't worry, it wasn't important' when asked to repeat themselves. Autistic people can face additional ableism if they have these conditions alongside being autistic but some ableist things are most relevant to autistic people:

'You don't look autistic' or 'You're only a little bit autistic' or 'Don't be so autistic' or 'Are you acting more autistic for attention?'

These are all phrases that someone might use to minimize your autistic identity; they reduce your needs to something they don't need to think about and include. This type of ableism relies on stereotypes about what autism is and can escalate to harmful behaviours. Ableism can push people to mask or camouflage their autism, to pretend their needs don't exist, or to seek out disingenuous social inclusion.

'If you could remove your autism, would you?' or 'If there were a cure for autism, would you take it?' or 'Autism can be cured by doing...' or 'If you do this it will make you less autistic'.

People focused on curing or eradicating autism see autism as an issue they need to fix or remove for autistic people. That really isn't the case. Science can show us what some of the causes of autism are or how we become autistic. This same science or even the harmful 'cures' that people develop can be used to make us feel bad about ourselves.[3] Instead of trying to change us, cure us, or remove the thing that is at the centre of everything we do, people should accept us for who we are. We can and should be accepted for who we are; we might not always immediately find people who do, but we can find people who love and accept us for our whole selves not discrete parts of us.

'They can't talk so don't need to be involved in decisions' or 'I never understand what they're trying to say' or 'We can't leave them on their own' or 'They'll never live a happy and independent life' or 'They're too slow to understand what we're talking about'.

Autistic people with additional needs in terms of their communication may face additional ableism as people treat them differently due to their differences in communication or

---

3    Some autism 'cures' promote the ingestion or use of chemicals that are toxic to the human body. They make us feel bad because they reiterate the idea of curing autism, and they can cause damage to us physically in some cases. Please don't take things that claim to cure autism: not only could they harm your body but there is no science to support any of the claims they make. Autism can't be cured but we can be supported.

expression. These groups include users of Augmentative and Alternative Communication (AAC), being non-speaking or situationally mute, and autistics with co-occurring conditions like a learning disability. This isn't okay. People shouldn't be treated differently because of the conditions or support needs that they have. This kind of ableism hurts people by setting up hierarchies of disability, deciding on those who can be treated reasonably and those who can be hurt. It can be used to abuse people by taking away their agency and their choice and relies on the fact that they may not be able to defend themselves.

Ableism can happen to any autistic person, but it might be more overt towards those who have 'obvious autistic behaviours or differences' like communication, stimming, or body movements. With my friends, I've referred to this as the 'kid-gloves-ableist-paradox'. When someone discloses that they are autistic, or if someone thinks of them as different, they might start treating the autistic person differently – talking to them as if they are a baby or child and reducing their agency or autonomy. 'Kid gloves' comes from the well-known phrase, which means treating someone carefully or delicately (often like an autistic meltdown or bomb about to explode), and 'ableist' because this kind of behaviour is ableist. The 'paradox' here is in whether someone will or won't treat you differently after finding out you're autistic. It could go either way, but often people will talk to you more slowly and be inclusive in ways you don't need. People could treat you normally, but if they're not sure how to (it really should be as easy as treating you as you should be treated), then they lean into treating you like a child.

Ableism means that some people don't think about our needs. Because of this, they don't help us live good lives. People might try to prevent disabled people from getting healthcare we need, or from accessing education that we want to pursue, or deny us jobs we're more than capable of doing. Ableism has been around for a long time, and disabled people have been treated badly for a long time. If you have dealt with ableism, you are not alone.

We know that there is nothing wrong with being disabled – the issue is getting other people to understand that. People sometimes forget that disabled people don't exist to be the good deed a non-disabled person gets to do that day. We can have pride in our disabilities and work together to advocate for the change we want and need to see in society. This connection – disabled people working together – forms the backbone of the disability rights movement. Together disabled people have united to fight back against the ableism and discrimination that disabled people have faced and to push for society to be more accessible.

## Support at school, college, and university: what helps and what doesn't

Each person will have a different experience of education dependent on a few factors that impact every person who goes to school, college, or university. Your experience can be influenced by the support you receive, where you're taught, how well the teaching matches your abilities or needs, and whether the people around you become friends or enemies. As much as our autistic experience is modulated and shaped by the environment we're in, it is also shaped by the people in it. Inclusive spaces can be supported by inclusive people, but they can also become spaces we try to escape when faced with people who make those spaces impossible to be in.

A common struggle for autistic young people in education is being misunderstood, both by our teachers and by our peers. With these misunderstandings often come bullying, isolation, and exclusion. None of these things support accessing an education that meets an individual's needs, nor should they be an inevitability for autistic children and young people. Unfortunately, bullying is often treated as something of an inevitability if you are autistic, marginalized, or simply different. Our social structures are set up to value some people over others and denigrate those who deviate from a supposed norm or ideal.

## College, university, or something else?

In the UK, some colleges offer only further education qualifications, and some colleges offer a mix of further and higher education qualifications. Further education qualifications offered by colleges are either:

- level 2 (GCSEs graded 4–9, intermediate apprenticeships, or level 2 NVQs, for example) or
- level 3 (A levels, advanced apprenticeships, International Baccalaureate (IB), level 3 NVQs, or T levels).

Other countries may use different definitions for what education looks like as you progress into adulthood and post-school leaving qualifications – there is a lot of national and regional variation in qualifications. These different qualifications and levels do translate across countries but can get a bit confusing. Education establishments will clearly outline what qualifications or proficiency levels are required for entry to these international equivalents.

Sixth forms and sixth-form colleges in the UK may focus on A levels or IB, taking a more academic focus, while further education colleges often offer a blend of vocational and technical routes. Due to the nature of how academic qualifications diverge from technical or vocational-based courses (e.g. the difference between history and hairdressing) these courses are taught in different establishments. This is mainly about the facilities: history books can easily be in any room, but salon sinks are a bit tougher to fit into your standard classroom.

Universities and higher education institutions (HEIs) offer level 4 and above qualifications with each year of university near enough equivalent to a level of qualification in a three-year undergraduate course. Universities courses include bachelor's degrees, Master's degrees, doctorates (these can be research-focused or profession-focused), and shorter courses focused on professional development. Typically, university teaching might be in person or via distance learning depending on the course structure. The level of qualification is used to help distinguish what someone has achieved with their studies and offers a system to help cross-reference the degrees and qualifications from different countries.

Examples of the different levels and what they mean in the UK are as follows:

- Level 4 qualifications typically indicate a higher level of understanding than level 3 qualifications, which are normally associated with the qualifications received when you leave school. These might be a higher apprenticeship, certificate of higher education (CertHE), or higher national certificate (HNC).
- Level 5 qualifications include foundation degrees, which are equivalent to two-thirds of a bachelor's (undergraduate) degree.
- Level 6 qualifications are what is awarded at the end of an undergraduate degree, typically called a bachelor's degree. These might be a Bachelor of Science (BSc) or a Bachelor of Arts (BA), which can be with or without honours. Undergraduate degrees aren't simply awarded with a pass or fail: grades are grouped into first (above 70%), upper second or 2:1 (60–70%), lower second or 2:2 (50–60%), third (45–50%), pass (40–45%), and fail (below 40%). Some subjects have specific abbreviations due to their structure (these are subjects like engineering, which uses BEng).
- Level 7 qualifications relate to postgraduate degrees, which include integrated Master's (an undergraduate degree combined with a Master's degree), Master's degrees like a Master of Science (MSc) or Master of Arts (MA), postgraduate diplomas, and postgraduate certificates.
- Level 8 qualifications are normally doctorate awards, which are generally labelled as a Doctor of Philosophy (PhD or DPhil). A doctorate is normally a pass or fail,

and if you pass the viva (a spoken presentation and scrutiny of your research), you might need to make no corrections, minor corrections, or major corrections to your final thesis (your research write-up).[4]

## Choosing what subject to study and where

The rest of this chapter dives into university, which is also termed as higher education, tertiary education, or a university college depending on where you are in the world. It is a route a lot of people take, particularly if it links to a specific career path or if they want to further pursue an academic interest, at least in a formal way. Continuing education isn't for everyone; some people make it through school and decide that is as far as they want to go. If you're interested in pursuing an education at university this chapter offers up some advice from my (nearly) three degrees' worth of experience to help you navigate this new space. If this chapter isn't for you, you might want to skip ahead to the employment chapter, which isn't just about 'traditional' full-time paid work as it covers all the different routes and paths that someone might choose to take.

Choosing the right level and pathway you want to take through your study of a subject or topic or career means making quite a few decisions. You may want to start by thinking about the subject you want to study. It could relate to the career you want to have, an area you have an interest in, or something you want to find out more about. I hadn't previously studied psychology before applying for and completing a BSc in psychology but knew it was something I would be interested in, partially because of my interactions with mental health services and partially because I wanted to understand human psychology better. I wouldn't usually suggest choosing

---

4   If you're not from the UK, or even if you are, this might all look a bit complicated. It is a little bit! The main point is to show that education can go through multiple paths and there are many steps you can take – if you want to, that is.

a topic to study because of bad experiences in the area: while this could be an impetus to learn more about it, enjoyment is a better motivator. Wanting to be part of revolutionary reform to psychiatry turned out to be quite different to studying the breadth and depth of psychology.

For you, it might be more straightforward. You might have an interest in pharmacy, accounting, nursing, or other vocational subjects, or perhaps you have an interest in literature, computer science, or microbiology that you want to pursue further. While it does help to have a clear goal or direction for what you want to study, not everyone does. We can normally work these things out by ourselves, by talking to career advisors, friends, family, or those who have been to university. Generally, university is a way of teaching a topic in greater depth with the added opportunity to go down the rabbit holes of your choosing. You can choose the things that you want to learn about and decide whether you want a career from it or 'just' the experience of learning. This, of course, would be easier to do if education were universally free and wasn't treated like a product, but until we get to that point choices about education do have to be strategic and focus on a degree's 'usefulness'.

University isn't like learning in a school or college as they generally must follow a national curriculum or a course as outlined by an exam board. Universities have much more freedom in how they shape their courses by making use of the skills and knowledge of staff that work there to lead on research areas that they focus on. When looking at which university you want to attend it is important to look at what research is done in your chosen subject alongside the practical aspects like location, facilities, and support. Some courses might have a bit more structure if they are accredited by a professional body,[5] so there might be similarities across some courses with

---

5    My psychology course had to teach certain topics at certain times to be accredited by the British Psychological Society.

the same name but then huge differences in other areas of the course.

## Location, location, location

Once you figure out what you want to study you then need to decide where to study. Thinking about where to go has several facets to it. The physical location can be important: whether the university is spread out over a city or on a self-contained campus, what the transport links are like, how far away from your family it is, and whether there are lots of green spaces or lots of buildings. To help figure this out I suggest going to different universities for open days or campus tours. Shifting it from being an abstract on-screen imagining to an in-person experience can help you to envisage yourself there (or not), grasp what studying might be like, and what the university or college does well.

The physical geography of a space is just as important as the social geography; well, either that or I don't know as much about geography as I pretend to. The social opportunities available, things to do in the university's city, the support you can access, and how comfortable you feel are all important factors that shouldn't be overlooked. For sporty people, which is definitely not me, things like sports facilities and societies are really important. For studious people, a good library, good careers support, societies that explore subjects or interests in depth, and the strength of the research focus of a university are all essential.

Whether you want to get as far away from family as possible, stay close to home, or somewhere in the middle, you still need a feasible way to get home by plane, train, bus, or car, or at the very least to be able to get yourself and your belongings to university. So, choosing somewhere that you can easily travel to from home is a key consideration. Some universities are remote, there aren't big towns built up around them, or they aren't well connected to rail and road. Others practically take over towns, sprawling out with buildings, accommodation, and students around every corner and with many modes of getting anywhere. Some towns and cities also have more than one university in them catering to tens of thousands of students who have shaped the city to fit their migratory needs.

When choosing a university, you ideally want to like the area in which you will be spending a few years of your life. This is something you can research as much as you want to, but sometimes the answer only comes when you visit a place. Figuring out if it feels like a good fit, whether you like the university, and whether you feel like there are opportunities there is one of the harder-to-describe parts of university. Some people look beyond the university itself for somewhere they can get a part-time job, somewhere with political views that align with theirs, or an ethos that fits with theirs. It's hard to describe when the vibe feels right, but you will feel it.

**Your sensory needs, your surroundings, and your support**
Where you live will probably be somewhere you spend a lot of time while at university. You might hear horror stories about housemates or hear about people making friends for life – both these things can happen.

Everyone warns you about a student kitchen, the need to bleach everything, mould growing its own mould children, smells no one can distinguish, and empty alcohol bottles collected in precarious piles for recycling. It's generally an assault on the senses and can result in failed attempts at executive function (I found it difficult to plan or cook meals in a dirty shared kitchen). Your sensory sensitivities or ability to stomach this type of kitchen or just whether you want to cook or not can determine what decision you come to about self-catered or catered accommodation at university. On the one hand, catered accommodation means you don't have to cook, and the menu can be predictably reliable. On the other hand, the menu might not include favourite foods, can be expensive, and you might prefer the autonomy of cooking for yourself.

Where you eat and cook is one part of the equation; you also must factor in your room, teaching spaces, and private or public study areas. These are all places you will spend a fair amount of time in, so it is essential that you know what you can control and put in place the support you need for the things you can't. Some people might thrive in bustling accommodation, and others might need somewhere that isn't in the middle of everything so that they can rest and relax. You get to choose where you live at university, so you can choose bustling and loud or quiet and out of the way if you want to.

Figuring out your access needs and how to communicate them to others is another key part of figuring out your autistic identity. Knowing how to articulate aspects of yourself so you aren't misunderstood is extremely difficult when you first start describing everything. Universities have support and departmental staff who can support you with reasonable adjustments and figuring out how to make university fit your needs. This might be a disability advisory or support service, personal tutor, wellbeing team, student services, or independent mentors or supports. The staff who can support you may span both professional and academic services. Once you find the people who can help you get the support you need, the process is much smoother, hopefully anyway, but not always.

It might take you some time to work out how to communicate your access needs, what to ask for, and who to share them with. I want to stress that this feeling is completely normal as it is a process that evolves and grows with you; growth can feel uncomfortable. You might share some needs that you don't always need support with or learn more about your needs and change what you want to share. University is incredibly different to the learning and teaching you may have previously experienced so having an adjustment period is normal. When you do find supports or ideas that you want to share, write them down – don't think you'll remember them for later! Trust me, your future self will appreciate everything you note down from 'one question at a time' through to 'needing explicit information and instructions'. Noting down this information, whether it changes or stays the same, will help spark some of the conversations you might have about explaining what autism means for you and the support you need in your education, socializing, or environment.

## Applying

University and some college course applications are made through the national system in your country; other applications are made directly to the institution. Admissions procedures will differ depending on the university and course, and some applicants may be asked to sit exams or attend interviews. You can apply with your grades and written statements about why you want to attend that university or why you chose the specific course. You might find specific methods that work best for you or depending on where you choose to apply.

Autism is labelled a disability through various pieces of equality legislation across the world. This isn't a bad thing: it means that colleges and universities have a duty to make reasonable adjustments to their procedures so that they are accessible to autistic applicants. Procedures should be accessible for you and inclusive of your needs from the initial application all the way through to when you get there.

## Socializing, making friends, and finding yourself

Everyone who goes to university wants to make friends, or at least that was the sense that I got while there. We all want or need someone to talk to about this big new thing we're doing together that is tough at times. Making friends at university isn't easy, and it is something that everyone struggles with to some extent or another. We all go to university knowing no one, and we're all shepherded around shared spaces (lectures, accommodation, welcome events, and society introductions) until friendships start to form. These friendships can start tenuously, but can grow in depth through shared interests, shared understanding, and bonding over shared experiences. Autistic people might need a bit more support to figure out how to navigate this newness; with new locations, new routines, and new people who don't know your history it can be difficult to make friends. We might not have the social scripts to get us through these new types of interactions or spaces as well as some of our other rehearsed interactions. On the other hand, that much newness and a chance for a fresh identity can make things easier.

I always found university much easier when it came to making friends than school. School always felt so forced, especially with 'friendships of convenience'. We were friends because we shared the same space five days a week and didn't bully each other – that was the basic premise of school friendships for me. University enables you to meet other people who are interested in the same things as you. They might study the same course or be in the same department or be in some of your modules or lectures. It also enables you to meet others with the same hobbies as you. You can meet people through societies, by getting involved in what the university does, at social events, or through working together academically or professionally.

It might feel overwhelming because you move from somewhere where you know pretty much everyone to somewhere where you know pretty much no one. It is a little scary, but the reality is also that this is a chance to meet so many new people and many will have similar interests to you. At university, if you and enough people share a passion for a special interest, you can set up a club or society to chat about it and share your info-dumping with others. Societies are one of the best parts of university; many are organized through the student's union and offer structure to socializing centred around one common topic.

## Support at university

My best advice for getting the support you need at university is unfortunately to make the best use of the bureaucratic system around you. It means extra form filling other students don't have to do, being proactive in reaching out for support, and asking for help earlier than when you think you need it. These aren't easy things to do and aren't things anyone should have to do, but they are what we must go through to have a chance at an equitable education.

### Formalized schemes for support

At university in England, this often consists of accessing Disabled Students Allowance (DSA), which offers support packages that are tailored to your needs. DSA isn't always easy to access: you must fill in forms, find medical evidence, and be assessed for your needs to then get everything put into place. Unlike a lot of other supports available to disabled people, DSA is truly on the side of you, the disabled person. This can feel weird if you're used to fighting for accessibility and inclusion. The people working within the support system want you to get the support that you need, but they need to work within a system that doesn't always make that a smooth journey.

DSA opens up a whole wealth of support that can offer a safety net for when things get difficult. I couldn't have made my way through university without my specialist mentor, study skills support, the software that made learning more accessible to me, or even just having someone who could advocate for my needs when I couldn't. For many students, DSA is part of a package of support that makes studying more equal. Reasonable adjustments are there to offer support to mitigate the challenges that can occur when studying while disabled.

In other countries or regions, there might be different arrangements for support at university. Sometimes this can depend on your specific university; sometimes it depends on your course. Support can also be dependent on the arrangements at a local or national level and your student status (whether you are a home or international student). Generally, your rights to access support, which can be either direct or indirect adaptations to your education, will be covered by disability, education, or civil rights legislation in your country of study. Most, if not all, universities will have disability services with staff who are there to support you with determining and accessing the support you need. You are entitled to an education that meets your needs and supports you to flourish in education. You deserve more than to receive an education that you are not fully able to access.

## Other support at university

I strongly recommend registering with your university's disability support service. It's something you can do when enrolling at university or at any point in your university journey. It can feel scary sharing that you're autistic and the needs that you have, but if you don't share these things, it is so much harder to get support if you need it, when you need it. When you do register with a university disability support service you will typically be assigned a disability advisor who can support you with queries related to your access needs and inclusion processes at university. These advisors are used to answering all kinds of questions for a range of different disabilities and supporting students with the questions that might come up for different subjects and processes.

Your university might have a way for you to concisely express your access needs and reasonable adjustments that you need to help you thrive in your education through a document, form, or conversation. It is useful for this to be shared with those who support disabled students in your school, department, or faculty (different universities use different terms for this). In terms of teaching and pastoral support, you should share your needs with those you interact with in your teaching and learning so they can enact the support you need.

This includes your personal tutor and module leads for your teaching, but you get to choose who sees what information about you. Sharing a concise document outlining your needs cuts through a lot of the red tape. It can be a lot easier than having to share a diagnosis document or doctors' notes. I mean, easier in terms of you getting to control the information shared, in the language that you choose.

Having something that is easily recognized as a document about your educational needs can have more power to convince staff of your needs. It outlines that these are *needs* – they aren't flimsy wants that can be ignored. Although some people might prefer to know about your specific disabilities and conditions, I've found it is more useful to talk about my specific support needs. People don't need to know the condition that necessitates the support. Wanting to know about your diagnosis can feel intrusive, especially if it then prompts someone to think about the way they might generically support someone with the same diagnosis. What works for someone who shares similar experiences might not work for you. Being specific about your needs should help reduce the generalizations that people make.

Your university might offer you support through:

- extra time on exams
- alternative assessments, especially if spoken presentations or group projects spike your anxiety
- extensions to deadlines for assignments
- consideration of your processing and writing differences when marking or assessing your work
- reasonable adjustments in teaching design and delivery.

These are all thoughts to get you started, but you might have different things that you prefer as support. Some of these adjustments are easily facilitated by existing university structures, and some might be new to them.

## Questions to consider when asking about support

Universities are putting more work into their disability support services; it is worth considering what support is available when looking at which university to attend.

1. Ask about autism-specific initiatives that the university has in terms of student support. You can also ask about any support for other conditions you have and examples of support that other students might have accessed. Knowing what support is available can help you to picture what support you need. Many universities are focusing on autism and mental health as a major part of their disability support so may have specific programmes they have developed or staff with elevated levels of understanding about autism.

2. Ask about what study skills resources there are. Most university librarians work closely with the disability support service, careers advice service, university departments, and centralized support services. Many have knowledge and expertise relevant to skills needed for subjects, can offer general and personalized support, and might be specifically trained to support disabled students.

3. Ask about which staff are there to support you and the roles that exist at the university generally and within your department specifically. Knowing who to go to and for what is incredibly underrated – it's very useful to know the structures and pathways. Knowing this before things go wrong or you reach a crisis is something that can make getting out of crisis a bit easier.

4. Ask about the type of support that people have received previously if you don't know what you might ask about for yourself. Having a few examples to support you in figuring out what you might want yourself is a great way of building understanding of what is available and what has helped others. This is something I didn't

realize would be as useful as it is, mainly because any time I was asked what I needed as support, I didn't have experiences to draw upon. In my case, support either hadn't happened or hadn't helped me, so I couldn't say what I needed, just what I had negative experiences of.

## Making your next steps

Figuring out what to do once you get to the other side of university, whether that is with a degree or without one, can be daunting. It's not enough that we achieve the degree itself with all the seemingly insurmountable mountains of essays, exams, presentations, and dissertations or theses that involves: we must have a plan for what comes next.

For some people, this might be a job or graduate scheme where they get to focus on something specific or work within a company to find out what type of work they want to do. For others, it might be taking some time to think about what the right thing for them looks like and not necessarily having it all figured out. No matter what, once you start looking and thinking about the direction you want to go in, there is an overload of information.

Moving cities, starting a new job, making new friendships, and leaving what might retrospectively feel like the safe routine of university, are all options open to you. The next chapter is all about one of these options – employment.

# Moving on to Employment

Apprenticeships, Internships, Part Time, and
Full Time – What Do They All Mean?

Moving on from education can be difficult, as often it is one of the most supported environments you will experience, that is, once you get the right support put in place. Leaving these supportive environments by ageing out of services (e.g. graduating from school or education) or by choice and moving into the 'adult world' often means employment as a next step. Employment is generally the next expected life stage for many people after they achieve the level of education they choose (high school, college, or university, for example). While employment in its various forms is much easier said than done when it comes to autistic people, it can, when properly supported, offer continued learning and the opportunity to find out what you are good at.

When school or university or any pathway through education ends it can be quite worrying. You're simultaneously being told you have all of these options open to you, you have to make decisions, and you're suddenly an adult. It means moving on from the familiar routines you may have had for most of your life so far, which can be hard even if school and education were not completely positive experiences for you. Some people don't leave education when school ends and might opt for university, a college course, or an apprenticeship.

Statistics for autistic people in employment are not encouraging: compared with the numbers for other disabilities, autistic people have the lowest levels of full-time or part-time employment. The Office of National Statistics report on 'Outcomes for disabled people in the UK: 2021' found that while 81.6 per cent of non-disabled people are employed only 29.0 per cent of autistic people are in any form of employment.[1] There are a few possible reasons for these relatively low levels of employment:

1. Some autistic people are working and are in jobs. These jobs might be roles they enjoy and are supported in; others might have jobs that don't fully match their skills or enable them to use their capabilities to the full.

2. Some autistic people are seeking work but struggle to get a job or stay in a job. This is due to inaccessible recruitment processes and workplaces without reasonable adjustments.

3. Some autistic people aren't currently focused on employment because they are studying, volunteering, looking after others, or they're looking after their health. These are all possible reasons why someone might be of 'working age' but not in employment or seeking employment.

4. Some autistic people might choose never to work as they may have health or support needs that can make employment more complicated for them, or they may not be able to work. Capitalism doesn't make this option easy or feasible for most people, and, importantly, someone should not be valued less if they cannot or do not work.

5. Although these statistics focus on working-age adults, some people might be retired. This could be through early retirement, medical retirement, or they've reached retirement age in their country.

---

1 Sparkes, I., Riley, E., Cook, B., & Machuel, P. (2022). Outcomes for disabled people in the UK: 2021. Office for National Statistics. Retrieved 29 June 2022, from https://www.ons.gov.uk/peoplepopulationandcommunity/healthandsocialcare/disability/articles/outcomesfordisabledpeopleintheuk/2021

Whichever group you fit into might be the group you are in for the moment or for a while; some people stay in one group for their whole life and others move between these different groups. Getting a job seems impossible or unlikely, especially if you are repeatedly told how unlikely it is for autistic people to have a job. I'm probably not helping here with my stark statistics. The good news is that many organizations and employers are finally listening and looking at how to include autistic people in the workplace through alterations to job applications, interview and onboarding processes, and all other reasonable adjustments to keep autistic people in employment.

Many organizations now run schemes that provide entry-level roles for autistic people that provide a supported transitionary space to gain work experience with employers who have additional training about autism. Depending on where you live and the interests that you have there might be employability schemes that could be the perfect fit for you, though it might take a little searching to find them. If an autism-specific scheme isn't for you there are also employability schemes that specifically focus on getting disabled people into employment that matches their needs, or schemes aimed at other identity characteristics like age.

## What does applying for a job look like?
Applying for jobs can seem like a big task, and it is, but that means it can be split into smaller tasks to make it more achievable. The first thing to decide is what kind of job you want to do. You can discuss this with friends or family to explore what kind of jobs there are (team-based, creative, labour-intensive, thinking-based, or serving others) and the sectors that you could work in.

Another option is to take career aptitude tests online which show you the options that might be aligned with your skills and interests, but these aren't an exact science and often don't show all the different kinds of jobs you can do. No test I've taken to work out what I might be able to do has shown any of the jobs I've done so far, but they have tended to show areas or careers that I'm interested in. Maybe they're not a complete waste of time, but they are a bit like career horoscopes so I'm not sure how much weight to give them.

Once you have an idea of what you want to do as a job or what you want work to look like for you, the next step is turning ambition into something you do rather than something you hope for. To do this involves looking for jobs that are recruiting. Long gone are the days of handing in a CV to a shop or office; now we're in a time of highly competitive recruitment where 'all you need' is to be better than another person. Once you have found a job you are interested in, you will need to apply for it in the way specified in the job listing. This may involve filling out an application form, or sending them your CV and a cover letter, tailoring both to fit the role and to show how your skills are a good match for the job description. With luck, you may get an interview. It's a process that goes on and on until either you get it right or someone chooses you for a role.

## Reasonable adjustments for applying

I've experienced recruitment with success a few times across different types of roles and areas, which has given me the perspective to think back on all the different jobs I've applied for, and all the time I've spent filling out applications, changing my CV, looking over job descriptions, in some cases making it through to interview and in others being second best. Many of these stages, steps, and aspects can be barriers to employment when you're autistic or have another disability. We know this shouldn't be the case, because that would mean discrimination, either direct or indirect, intended or unintended. But we still know it happens, and we still worry about it happening to us if we share the parts of ourselves that others might choose to victimize.

Before COVID-19 reshaped the employment sector it felt as if autism and neurodiversity were the next frontiers to be explored in employment's focus on diversity. So many discussions that I had been a part of before the working-from-home and hybrid revolution were focused on the value that autistic and similarly neurodivergent people could add to a business.

## Inclusive practices in the era of inclusion

Inclusive recruitment can involve more work to put into place the processes that people need, but has the benefit of giving those who may not have previously applied a chance at a job. Once the processes are developed, they become the standard way of working and aren't extra work – they're just how it's done. Asking for what you need is a right – you should not be made to feel like a burden.

Recently, the employment sector has been under increasing scrutiny concerning its diversity practices. While the primary focus has been on getting society to reflect on the systematic and institutional racism that perseveres, diversity has a wider remit. Diversity includes disability, gender expression, sexual orientation, and any other characteristics that people have that society uses to marginalize them (people aren't in themselves marginalized but are marginalized by societal 'norms'). Many changes are needed within organizations to ensure that equality, diversity, and inclusion (EDI) are embedded in their practices. Good progress has been made in some areas of organizational EDI but others remain stagnant.

## What does inclusive recruitment look like for autistic people?

Often only small changes are needed, but with so many steps to recruitment it can feel like a daunting task to tackle all the areas in which inequality can grow.

## Job descriptions

Language that points to specific tasks without room for reasonable adjustments, unclear descriptions, and asking for
qualifications and experience without linking them to the role
are all examples of exclusionary practice. Phrases like 'fast-
paced environment' may not gel well with someone who is
methodical, and process driven, as often process is thrown out
the window when the pace picks up. Additionally, stating that
parts of the role must be done in a certain way does not benefit
any business: systems can always be improved and changed
to reach their best. Ultimately, what works for one colleague
might slow down another. Finally, asking for a degree excludes
many candidates who may have relevant experience gained
through professional and personal roles, and diminishes what
they may have mastered by taking the 'alternative' path.

To make job descriptions and person specifications inclusive, those writing them should focus on the key 'deliverables'
of the role: what they will be doing and what they will need to
know to do it. Using clear, concise, and factual language rather
than buzzwords helps everyone – it cuts through what can be
interpreted as grey and makes things black and white. Often
it is easier for people to use jargon to explain things quickly,
but that excludes those who might not know the jargon yet.

A job description and person specification are an organization's opportunity to show someone applying not only what
they're all about as a place to work but how they treat their
prospective employees. Recruitment and applying for roles
are often seen as the candidate or applicant having to sell
themselves to an organization, but it's a two-way street. We
want to work at places we can see ourselves being – places
that feel welcoming rather than workplaces that create an
unwelcoming vibe before we've even applied.

## Application stage

Depending on the size and type of organization that you're
applying to, there might be very different ways of applying.

Some organizations ask for a CV and cover letter, others might have an online application system, and others might use recruitment agencies. There are pros and cons to each of these.

If the company just asks for a CV and cover letter this can make things a little bit easier, but only if they're clear about what they want to be highlighted. Typically, in applications like this it's best to tailor your CV and cover letter to the job role and the person specification. Ensure your CV matches up with the experience and skills they are looking for. For cover letters, write in a systematic way addressing each of the points in the job specification rather than using a scattergun approach. Matching your skills and experience to those listed in the application materials reflects back to them what they want to see, and going methodically through the points they've highlighted can give you a structure for your application. This also makes it easier for those hiring to pick out the skills and competencies that they will be assessing and looking for in your application.

Job applications take huge amounts of time and effort to complete, and this shouldn't be underestimated when applying. Give yourself enough time to figure out how you want to write about yourself, how you want to answer questions, and how you feel you would be best represented. Sometimes if you're applying in the same field or for the same types of jobs you can reuse or at least repurpose some of what you have written or used before. This shortcut can help save time and form part of the learning process, but don't forget to change and personalize what you've written, and make sure you name the files appropriately. No one wants to have the regretful moment of sending a document only to realise its file name relates to a different company! Take time to check what you've written for spelling, grammar, and clarity, and how it aligns with the specific needs of the role you are applying for.

## Reasonable adjustments and access needs

Reasonable adjustments that can be made by your employers or those around you to support you at work include the following:

- Writing down instructions and tasks, especially after saying them aloud to you.
- Giving short, clear instructions rather than piling on multiple requests, questions, or instructions at once.
- Breaking down large tasks into smaller components, particularly if it is something new to you.
- Having a regular timetable of tasks to add structure to your working day.
- Asking that people make it clear if you are talking too long about a subject and providing a non-judgemental space for social differences.

You may also like to talk to your manager or HR team about seeing if they will arrange autism awareness training for all staff or just those you interact with or work with frequently. Training is typically offered by external companies and charities and could be something that will help your team understand your needs more, and in turn, lead to a more supportive workplace for you.

Asking for reasonable adjustments at work is something you can do at any stage of the process, from initial application all the way through to starting your job or once you get settled. You might know what to ask for from previous experiences, or it might be an iterative process of working out what you need in specific situations. If you need some help thinking about what reasonable adjustments you might want, you can talk to friends and family or have a look online. As part of the Discover Autism Research and Employment initiative, researchers have created an excellent toolkit[2] with examples of adjustments in different areas of work.

## When at work

Once you've secured a job and you've started work, the next thing to do is turn up each day, bring the parts of yourself that you want to bring to the job, and do as many of the tasks on your to-do list as possible each day. I won't promise it will always be easy: sometimes it might be fulfilling and at other times it might be exceedingly difficult.

There isn't as much advice to give here as I'd like: jobs are all so unique in how they work, at least beyond turning up, figuring out what to do that day, getting on with your tasks, having a break, finishing up, and then heading home. Mainly, it's just doing the things you have to do, ideally progressing in your career as you'd like (especially without comparing yourself too much to others), and with any luck making work friends and avoiding discrimination or burnout.

Employment can offer us the opportunity to pursue the interests that we have while getting paid for it, but sometimes it is just doing tasks to get paid so we can pursue our interests outside of work. Whichever it is for you, remember that you spend a fair chunk of your time at work so it should be somewhere you enjoy being, somewhere that provides benefits to you, and if you aren't happy, you can change jobs.

Trying to offer advice when the scope of employment is so incredibly vast isn't easy, but some tips might help across most types of work:

- You're unlikely to remember everything, so take notes to refer to and remind yourself of how tasks are done,

---

2   Heasman, B., Livesey, A., Walker, A., Pellicano, E., & Remington, A. (2020). DARE report on adjustments. Centre for Research in Autism and Education, Institute of Education, UCL, London, UK. Retrieved 13 October, from https://dareuk.org/dare-adjustments-toolkit

what tasks you have to do, and anything else you need to remember concerning people or processes.

- You might have a way of doing things, and your employer might have a preferred way of doing things. There might be room for changes to how things work, or your boss might be strict in how they like things done. Sometimes you can innovate in how things work, and sometimes doing things the way they've always been done is what causes the least fuss.

- Everybody makes mistakes,[3] but what's most important is learning from them. Dwelling on what went wrong can feel comforting to some extent, but moving forward, listening to feedback, and adapting to avoid making the same mistake again is generally the best way forward. People will forgive missteps when they see progress and shouldn't hold mistakes against you – we're only human after all.

- If you're not sure about something, ask. Some people are more open to questions than others, but I always see those with questions as looking for answers they genuinely need rather than intentionally pestering someone. You've probably heard that there are no silly questions (some are intentionally silly, at least I think so), so remember this when you're asking a question about something you're unsure of – you're asking because you don't know the answer!

---

3   Not to be all Hannah Montana about it but every single person will make a mistake at some point. It sounds a bit negative to think about it that way, but, honestly, no one can be perfect and please everyone with every single action they take.

# Part III

# Finding Out More

# Conclusions and
# Further Resources

As I've said before, the only thing all autistic people share is this diagnosis. That's a good thing for bringing us together but also means our experiences may only have a few intersecting threads and the rest are completely divergent. We might have similar struggles, but they aren't all the same; they're similar, but they're also uniquely ours. That means writing about all the different directions our lives can take is far from simple, especially as I've never really found generalizations that useful myself. Personally, I much prefer when things are specific, no matter how granular that detail is. I hope this book has shown you that you are not alone and that the struggles you may face are not struggles you have to face alone.

This final section of the book points you in the direction of some further resources, things to listen to, and things to read. Most of what I've collated is from autistic people, people who are otherwise neurodivergent, or disabled people. I hope these resources and directions provide some solidarity and relatability.

# Things to Listen to

**1800 Seconds on Autism**
This is a BBC sounds podcast hosted by Jamie Knight and Robin Stewart, who are both autistic adults. They cover topics related to autism and sometimes bring in additional guests to cover perspectives that they don't have experience with. Jamie and Robin offer their well-informed views on different topical ideas arising for autistic people with an episode of organized chaos (the chaos is typically organized by producer Emma Tracey, who occasionally peeks out from behind the scenes of the podcast) every month or when life allows the team to create episodes.

**21andsensory**
This podcast is hosted by Emily, an illustrator who manages to perfectly encapsulate neurodivergent life in her illustrations. Emily is autistic and has sensory processing disorder. Each episode she talks to a new neurodivergent guest and together they chat about neurodiversity, autism, and sensory processing. Emily provides the perfect space for each guest to dive into the things they find fascinating.

**Autism By Autistics**
Melissa and Sophie are both autistic autism researchers, and their podcast discusses different topics related to autism. Together they combine their personal autistic perspectives and their professional academic researcher perspectives to dig into some good old autistic discussion.

**Aut-Hour**
In this limited-series podcast hosted by Sara Gibbs, the author of *Drama Queen*, she chats with other autistic authors about their diagnosis, their writing, their life, and how all of these things interweave. This podcast is a great listen for those who want to find out a bit more about writing, publishing, and finding your niche as a creatively inclined autistic person. Guests on the podcast are a mixture of autistic people who have received a diagnosis at different points in their life and write in a variety of different fields from children's authors, journalists, comedy writers, and those who also work academically. These guests cover pretty much every base while providing a reading list of work created by autistic people.

## The Accessible Stall
This podcast is hosted by Emily Ladau and Kyle Khachadurian. They provide casual conversations and friendly arguments about both light and heavy disability topics. Although this podcast isn't explicitly about autism, it makes a great listen for those interested in wider discussions about disability.

## The Squarepeg Podcast
This podcast brings together guests who are all autistic people of marginalized genders (women, trans, and non-binary people) to talk through their lives, what they've found easy, and what hasn't been easy.

## Neurodiverging
The host of this podcast, Danielle, is an autistic parent with neurodivergent children. Through the podcast, Danielle dives into topics that she draws from her own life, some neurodivergent interests, and all things autism or ADHD. If you're interested in the intersection between the two, this podcast is for you.

## Sensory Matters
This podcast is presented by the Sensooli team (previously known as Chewigem) and brings together experts to talk about all things sensory to provide an affirmative space for sensory seekers, those who stim, and autistic people. The main audience is technically parents, carers, and professionals, but it is worth a listen for all things sensory focused.

# Things to Read

*All the Weight of Our Dreams: On Living Racialised Autism*, edited by Lydia X. Z. Brown, E. Ashkenazy, and Morénike Giwa Onaiwu
An anthology of 61 artistic and wordy works from autistic authors of colour. Taking the shape of short essays, poems, and a variety of creative methods, this is the first anthology that only centres around the work of autistic people of colour. It's a must-read, particularly with the whitewashing of so many of the narratives about autism and autistic people.

*The Spectrum Girl's Survival Guide: How to Grow Up Awesome and Autistic*, by Siena Castellon
If you want a bit more in terms of advice and support and you fit the demographic of autistic teen girl, then Siena's book is for you. Packed full of tips for tackling those firsts in life, Siena draws upon her own experience to help guide you through.

*Spectrum Women: Walking to the Beat of Autism*, edited by Barb Cook and Dr Michelle Garnett
If you're looking for something a little bit older than Siena's book and want to hear from autistic women who advocate for autistic people's rights, then this is for you. This book is packed with personal experiences, directions for you to head in yourself, and recommendations for where to find more resources.

*The Autism and Neurodiversity Self Advocacy Handbook: Developing the Skills to Determine Your Own Future*, by Barb Cook and Yenn Purkis
Keeping on that same topic of advocacy and, importantly, self-advocacy, some of the same authors from *Spectrum Women* have written about how to take what they've learnt about self-advocacy and activism and apply it to your own life. If you have every intention of turning a passion for autism into advocacy work or activism (as many autistic people have), then this is an essential text and starting point.

*Queerly Autistic*, by Erin Ekins
An essential guide for autistic LGTBIQ+ teens, covering all aspects of identity, relationships, and, crucially, safety. Not many people talk about the intersections of autism, gender, and sexuality, which makes Erin's book so necessary. It covers almost every question you might have and offers solidarity that many might not get in real life.

*We're Not Broken: Changing the Autism Conversation,* by Eric Garcia
Taking his experience in journalism and the 'often told by others history of autism', Eric flips that narrative to be told by autistic people, reframing what has often been about us to be by us. Eric focuses on autism in America and all the bits that the media has tended to get wrong. This book is a rallying cry for getting things about us right and for us to be the ones shouting about them rather than being shouted over.

*Drama Queen,* by Sara Gibbs
Sara is an incredible writer, wickedly witty comic, and someone who only found out she was autistic in her 30s, despite all the signs catalogued through family home videos. *Drama Queen* offers a trip down memory lane for one autistic brain (owned by Sara) and offers up a declaration that an autism diagnosis isn't the end of the world. Through an incredibly frank exploration of her memories and life, Sara shows just how long negative labels stick around until you peel them away with the healing magic of self-acceptance, love, and joy. Obviously, with an added laugh or two, and maybe a self-deprecating joke thrown in there for some fun.

*Stim: An Autistic Anthology,* edited by Lizzie Huxley-Jones
An incredible anthology of 18 pieces of short fiction, personal essays, and art created by autistic people that is edited by the fantastic Lizzie Huxley-Jones, who opened my eyes to the breadth and depth of autistic writing. This anthology was crowdfunded and features some people I am glad to call friends and the work of many I admire.

*Odd Girl Out,* by Laura James
This looks at life before an autism diagnosis and how, after diagnosis, things can change or stay the same. The book is written in a diary style, and Laura takes you along with her on her journey. I have often recommended this book to people trying to work out if they are autistic, or if they have just received a diagnosis.

*I Overcame My Autism and All I Got Was This Lousy Anxiety Disorder: A Memoir,* by Sarah Kurchak
If you appreciate witty writing and hearing from another Sarah, this book is a great read. Sarah's memoir covers her experience of navigating autism in Canada in the 1980s and 1990s, being different, and the intersections between autism and anxiety (of which there are many!).

*The Electricity of Every Living Thing,* by Katherine May
An anthology penned by Katherine as she processes her late autism diagnosis, and ultimately what it means for her past, present, and future. I've long been a fan of how Katherine strings together words in a way that feels almost poetic and as if there were no other way to write.

*Wintering*, by Katherine May
This is an additional memoir by Katherine and for me is an essential and brief bit of reading about burnout, depression, or your own personal 'winter' – how to recognize it, plan for it, and make it through to your own 'spring'.

*Diary of a Young Naturalist*, by Dara McAnulty
Dara is a prolific naturalist, advocating for climate action and protecting the world we live in rather than treating it as if our current actions are sustainable in any way. Taking the reader through the seasons of his native Northern Ireland, Dara talks openly about autism, the world we're in, and his interest in nature. It's a joy to see the beauty of nature through Dara's eyes.

*The Neurodiversity Reader*, edited by Damian Milton
*The Neurodiversity Reader* is a more academically focused text about neurodiversity written by neurodivergent people and researchers. The collection brings together work from thinkers within and beyond the neurodiversity movement who explore concepts related to neurodiversity. Building on the original inception of neurodiversity by Judy Singer, this book covers academic and practice interests in neurodiversity and how it has grown from an idea into a political movement.

*How to Be Autistic*, by Charlotte Amelia Poe
Charlotte's very personal memoir reveals the difficulty of navigating autism, mental illness, gender, and sexual identity. Looking back with hindsight, perspective, and sharply written chapters, Charlotte shows a side of autism that many who grew up in the 1990s and 2000s can relate to. I've never read such honest and evocative expressions of what anxiety feels like and how it creeps in like a monster that controls your life, paralysing you in its grip.

*Existing Autistic*, by Megan Rhiannon
The perfect zine for exploring autism. Megan uses her distinctive illustrative style and calming prose to describe her autistic existence with many themes and experiences that other autistic people can relate to. If you're more of a visual thinker or just want something you can easily dip in and out of, then *Existing Autistic* is perfect for finding language about autistic experiences in an accessible format.

*Neurotribes*, by Steve Silberman
Although Steve is not autistic himself, unlike the other authors listed here, *Neurotribes* is well recognized as one of the most thorough pieces of writing about the history of autism. It is the perfect piece of reading to help situate where we came from and how we got here.

*University and Chronic Illness: A Survival Guide*, by Pippa Stacey
Pippa is a chronically ill graduate and campaigner who writes from her own personal experience about navigating university while disabled. Instead of being a strict manual of how to be chronically ill at university, this book takes a gentler approach.

# Glossary

### Ableism
Discrimination on the basis of disability. In some cases, ableism is overt, such as the denial of life-saving organ transplants and the vast rates of unemployment among autistic adults. Ableist attitudes are often more subtle, but they are pervasive in our society. Framing or responding to disability in a negative way can be seen as ableism. Some examples are calling disabled people inspirational, segregating disabled people from non-disabled people, or treating interactions with disabled people like good deeds for non-disabled people. Disabled people can also be ableist about their own disability or other disabilities.

### Advocacy
Help you receive from someone else that enables you to get the care and support you need that is independent of whom you are seeking support from. An advocate might support you to express your needs and wishes, evaluate your options, and help you to make decisions about the options available to you. They do not make decisions for you; they help you to be heard and to understand the decisions that are being made.
An advocate might be useful to represent you when asking for support from your local council, healthcare provider, education provider, or employer. They may speak on your behalf or support you to speak. If you advocate for yourself this is called self-advocacy.

### Alexithymia
A condition in which someone struggles to recognize and understand their own internal states. These include emotions, drives like hunger and thirst, and physical bodily sensations. Someone with alexithymia may not 'feel' or process their internal states and may struggle to describe what they are thinking or feeling. Alexithymia may also be associated with differences in thinking style and imaginative processes. Typically, most people associate alexithymia with emotions and difficulty understanding or describing them.

### Allistic
Someone who is specifically not autistic. This term is similar to neurotypical, which refers to someone who is not neurodivergent.

## Anxiety

Anxiety is a condition that means you worry more than normal about things. Anxiety can be mild or very difficult to live with, and can change depending on the situation and support available. There are many causes for anxiety and different ways it can present; these don't always make sense to the non-anxious person.

## Ask Listen Do

A strategy staff working in the NHS might use to ask for your feedback. They will listen to what you are saying and try to implement what you say. For autistic people and those with learning disabilities, this structure can help when voicing your healthcare opinions.

## Attention deficit hyperactivity disorder (ADHD) or attention deficit disorder (ADD)

A term for a condition that someone can have alongside autism that centres around their attention and executive function. People who have ADHD might be more hyperactive, find concentrating on tasks difficult, or struggle with attention more than people who don't have ADHD. It is classed as a learning difficulty and is normally managed through good, individualized support and medication depending on the individual's preferences.

## Auditory processing disorder

A condition where the person has difficulty processing sound. They might take longer to understand speech, struggle to distinguish similar spoken words, be unable to concentrate when there is lots of noise, or hear music differently.

## Augmentative and Alternative communication (AAC)

An umbrella term that covers the different communication methods that may be used by people to communicate or aid communication. These can range from picture cards, symbols, and gestures to computer software that reads aloud what someone wants to communicate. This might also be called assistive and augmented communication. Typically, this refers to communication using non-verbal means or facilitated means of verbal communication.

## Autism, autism spectrum condition, and Asperger's syndrome

These are all the same condition but expressed differently. Autism is a condition that means someone is autistic. Autistic people process the world around them differently to non-autistic people. Someone who is autistic or has a diagnosis of autism/Asperger's is different in four areas. These are social interaction, communication, routines and repetition (social imagination), and sensory issues.

## Autism strategy

A national plan that explains what the government is doing to make sure that adults with autism get the help they need with things such as living independently and finding employment. Countries within the UK will have national autism strategies that inform local areas of the key priorities for autism services and policy. The autism strategy tells local councils and health services what they should do to help support autistic people. Many councils have their own autism strategy setting out what they will do to improve the lives of autistic adults in their area.

### Behaviour that challenges or behaviours of distress
When an autistic person is distressed, their behaviour often indicates their distress. The behaviour of those around them can be challenging for the autistic person, and the autistic person's behaviour can be challenging for those around them.

### Burnout
When an autistic person overstretches themself by doing too many tasks, too much socializing or making their brain work too hard, they can burn out. Burnout is similar to when you are ill, tired, and need a rest, but are unable to do so. The autistic person might not act like themselves because they aren't able to think as clearly as they did before the period of burnout started.

### Capacity
The ability to make your own choices and decisions. To make your own decisions, you need to be able to understand the impact of the decision, process the information involved in the decision, and communicate clearly what your choice is. You do not have to share your choice or decision verbally – you can share your choice non-verbally by writing or physically demonstrating your choice. A person might be judged to lack capacity because of a mental health problem, dementia, or learning disability; this is decided by an assessment of their mental capacity.

### Child and Adolescent Mental Health Services (CAMHS)
A service commissioned by the NHS in the UK to provide diagnostic and treatment services to children and young people up to the age of 18 with emotional or behavioural issues. CAMHS might be where someone receives an autism diagnosis, or may provide support with a mental health problem like anxiety or depression, or with behaviours like violence or aggression. People can be referred to CAMHS by different professionals in their life, and this might be one of many services that they use.

### Cognitive empathy
Understanding another person's perspective. Autistic people may struggle to empathize with non-autistic people in this way. Non-autistic people may struggle to understand an autistic person's perspective in a similar way.

### Communication
The way we understand and use language with others. Autistic people might show differences in understanding and expressing communication and language.

## Complex needs
A term that is used to describe someone who may have multiple conditions that require a higher level of support than someone without complex needs. An autistic person with complex needs might have co-occurring mental and physical health conditions that mean multiple people provide care and support to them so that they can enjoy their daily activities.

## Diagnostic and Statistical Manual of Mental Disorders (DSM)
The American Psychiatric Association's official manual used by professionals for the diagnosis of autism and other mental health conditions. The DSM is typically used by American health professionals to diagnose conditions. In 2013 the fifth edition (DSM-5 or DSM-V) was published.

## Diagnostic overshadowing
When you have a particular health condition or disability, some professionals may use this as an explanation for all health problems or symptoms you have. It often affects people with an existing learning disability or mental health condition and can mean that illnesses are missed or not treated properly.

## Disclosure
Autistic people can choose whether to tell other people that they are autistic and what that means for them. Some people choose not to disclose, and others choose whether to disclose depending on the situation they are in.

## Discrimination
The unjust or prejudiced treatment of people based on aspects of their identity. This might be because of prejudiced ideas about their race, age, gender, sexuality, or disability. Discrimination is an action; prejudice is the thought.

## Dyslexia
This condition means the individual has difficulty with reading and processing written information. Dyslexia is a neurodevelopmental condition that also means someone is neurodivergent.

## Echolalia
Repetition of another person's spoken words or repeating the same word over and over again. It can help someone process the information that they have been given.

## Education, Health and Care plan (EHC plan)
A legal document for a child or young person up to the age of 25 that outlines their specific education, health, and social care needs. This applies to children and young people in England. The plan is written and used as part of planning support that meets the needs of the child or young person in these areas. Importantly, an EHC plan should help a child or young person to achieve the things that they want to and provide the support to help them realize their ambitions. Previously EHC plans were called Special Educational Needs (SEN) Statements, but this was changed after the SEN reforms that occurred in 2014.

## Empathy

Empathy is our feelings and our understanding of other people's feelings. People refer to this as an ability to put yourself in another person's shoes or to understand their perspective alongside your own.

## Emotional empathy

When we understand another person's perspective and respond in an emotional way. Some people become sympathetic and show compassion when another person is distressed; other people show empathy by becoming distressed themselves.

## Executive function

Our ability to manage multiple tasks and responsibilities at once. Autistic people might struggle with one or more of the areas of executive function:

- Working memory – The thinking skill of holding information in your mind and being able to apply it to the situation you are in.

- Cognitive flexibility – The ability to think flexibly or have multiple approaches to the same problem. Autistic people may struggle with this due to liking routines and plans that do not change.

- Self-control – This aspect of executive function means controlling your actions and keeping track of what you are doing and how it relates to your goals.

## Expressive communication

The process or act of sharing information or messages with other people. This could be through talking, body language, writing, augmentative communication, or other ways of expressing what you want to say.

## Functioning labels

These are terms that were previously used to describe the autism spectrum. The terms high-functioning and low-functioning were used to describe autistic people who do not need too much support in their daily life or autistic people who need a lot of help and support from others in their daily life. As functioning is a subjective idea and can change depending on the environment, functioning labels were removed from descriptors about autism. If the environment is supportive and adapted to the needs of an autistic person, they may need less support.

## Hyper-focus

Highly focused attention on a task or activity that lasts an extended period of time. When someone hyper-focuses they concentrate on something so intently that they lose track of everything else going on around them.

## Impairment

A physical or mental health problem caused by an injury, illness, or condition that impacts your daily life. Impairment is the term used when discussing the social model of disability.

## Inclusion
The concept that disabled people and those who are different from the 'norm' should be integrated with their non-disabled peers. Inclusion is achieved by inclusive acts and practices that integrate people into activities, communities, and spaces.

## Info-dump or info-dumping
This is when an autistic person shares a lot of information at one time, normally 'dumping' a lot of 'information' about their special interest on/ to someone. Info-dumping is normally done enthusiastically, because it is an autistic person sharing their special interest, and might not fit the social situation it is being shared in. Essentially the practice of info-dumping is an expression of autistic joy shown through the sharing of information that has been catalogued about a special interest.

## International Statistical Classification of Diseases and Related Health Problems (ICD-11)
The manual created by the World Health Organization that enables a worldwide standard for diagnosis of health conditions and enables healthcare providers to develop statistics about different conditions across geographical regions.

## Interaction
How we relate to and socialize with other people. Autistic people may differ in the ability to understand social behaviour and the feelings of others, which informs the development of friendships and relationships.

## Learning difficulty
Unlike a learning disability, a learning difficulty does not affect intellect (learning disabilities have been labelled as intellectual disabilities in medical understanding). Examples of learning difficulties are dyscalculia, dysgraphia, dyslexia, dyspraxia, and language and social communication disorders.

## Learning disability
A learning disability is a reduced intellectual ability that may result in difficulty with everyday activities or taking longer to develop new skills. Learning disabilities are lifelong and can be mild, moderate, or severe. With the right support people with learning disabilities can lead independent lives. Some people can be autistic, have a learning disability, or both.

## Masking
Masking or camouflaging is when an autistic person acts in a way to appear less autistic or not autistic at all. They may change how they look, how they talk, and their behaviours. Too much masking can lead to burnout.

## Medical model of disability
The medical model of disability says people are disabled by their impairments or differences. Under the medical model, these impairments or differences should be 'fixed' or changed by medical or other treatments, even when the impairment or difference does not cause pain or illness.

## Meltdown

A meltdown is a response to an overwhelming situation. The response can be very loud and sometimes physical. The person needs time to recover and should not be laughed at for having a meltdown. Meltdowns can involve self-injurious behaviour, expressing feelings of distress, difficulty with communication, and disorientation.

## Mental health problem

These are problems with the way you think, feel, and react, which affect your ability to cope with life, make choices, and relate to other people. People may feel these things for a brief period or may need to seek support from a doctor if their symptoms persist for a long time or get worse. There are many different types of mental health problems, including depression, anxiety, eating problems, and other issues with emotions or behaviour. These can be treated in a variety of different ways and may last a long or short time.

## Neurodevelopmental condition

Anything relating to or involving the growth and development of the brain or central nervous system. It is an overarching term that means brain differences that last a lifetime.

## Neurodivergent

Someone who experiences a condition that means they are not neurotypical.

## Neurodiversity

Neurodiversity is the idea that the way we think is not always the same; people's brains work in different ways to each other. This recognizes that all variations of human neurology should be respected as another way of being, and that neurological differences like autism and ADHD are the result of natural variations in our genes. Just as we accept biological diversity (biodiversity), we should accept neurological diversity.

## Neurotypical

Someone who is not autistic and does not have any other neurodevelopmental condition or neurodivergency. A person who is neurotypical has a brain that works in a 'typical' way, and they are not neurodivergent.

## Peer support

The practical and emotional help and support that people who have personal experience of a particular health condition or disability can give each other, based on their shared experience. People support each other as equals, one-to-one or in groups, either face-to-face, online, or on the telephone.

## Prejudice

Preconceived ideas about someone based on their identity characteristics rather than the truth. People are pre-judged due to the beliefs that someone holds about the group that they belong to. This could be based on their race, sex, gender, age, religion, or disability. Prejudice is the thoughts that people have and discrimination is the act based on these thoughts.

### Reasonable adjustment
Changes that public services, buildings, education providers, and employers must make so it is possible for people with disabilities to use a service or do a job. These changes include things like adjusting your working hours or providing you with a special piece of equipment to do the job. It is against the law to discriminate against you because you have a disability.

### Receptive communication
The comprehension or understanding of spoken and written communication or gestures. It is the communication you receive from others.

### Routine
The order in which you do something and when you do it. This grouping of tasks can be big, or it can be small. Some autistic people have very strict routines that they like to stick to. Their routine is predictable and helps them to manage anxiety.

### Sensory processing and sensitivity
Sensory processing is how we take in and perceive sensory information. This may include hyper (high) or hypo (low) sensitivity to the five senses we know well, as well as additional senses we might not know quite as well – balance (vestibular), spatial awareness (proprioception), and internal bodily awareness.

Hyperreactive sensory sensitivity is when your senses are overly reactive. For sound this might be loud noises causing pain, quiet noises being louder for you than other people, and hearing every noise and not being able to disengage from the different sounds.

- Hyporeactive sensory sensitivity is when your senses are underreactive. For sight this might mean not being bothered about bright lights or not noticing things that other people see. You might need more sensory input to meet the same level of input experienced by others who aren't hyporeactive.

- Sensory seeking is when you seek out input; generally this is because extra input is joyful or makes you happy. This might be something someone does while stimming or when they are hyporeactive.

- Sensory aversive is when you avoid sensory input, perhaps because it is painful or overwhelming. This might be something someone feels or does when they are sensory hyperreactive.

### Sensory regulation
Our ability or inability to process the external sensory world and our internal senses. This might be done by stimming, seeking out sensory input, avoiding sensory input, or changing the environment around us to fit our sensory needs.

### Shutdown
Shutdowns are like meltdowns but are not as visible or loud. A person may withdraw instead of being their usual self.

**Special interest**
An intense and passionate level of focus on things of interest or a specific subject, for example, a game or TV show, a type of animal, a type of machine, or a country. Special interests are varied and bring the person joy.

**Social care**
Any help that you need, such as personal care or practical assistance, to live your life as comfortably and independently as possible, because of age, illness, or disability. This assistance and care is provided by family members or paid carers who support you at home or in a care facility.

**Social model of disability**
What makes someone disabled is not their impairment or difference, but barriers in the world around them. These barriers may be physical, such as lack of access to a building or lack of suitable toilets. Barriers are also created by people's attitudes to disability, and their assumptions about what disabled people can and cannot do. Removing these barriers creates equality and enables people to have independence, choice, and control over their lives.

**Social Stories™ by Carol Gray**
A Social Story™ describes a situation, skill, or concept in terms of relevant social cues, perspectives, and common responses in a specifically defined style and format. The goal of a Social StoryTM is to share accurate social information in a calm and reassuring manner that is easily understood by its audience.

**Stigma**
A set of negative and often unfair beliefs that a society or group of people have about a topic. These might be the 'first thoughts' that tend to be negative about something like a disability, ethnicity, accent, appearance, job, interests, or belongings.

**Stimming**
Stimming is short for 'self-stimulatory' behaviour. Stimming can be a repetitive movement, repeating words, hand movements, or making noises. Some stims are barely noticeable, and some are very visible. Stimming behaviours are a way of self-regulating and shouldn't be stopped or reduced as they are an autistic person's way of managing a situation.

**Stim toy**
An object used for stimming or fiddling with when a person might be feeling anxious. Stim toys come in a range of different types and can include fidget spinners, Playdoh, tangles, pens, soft toys, and balls. Each person's preference is unique and personal; using their preferred stim toy can help them to feel comfortable and support them to engage in the situation they are in.

**Supported living**
A type of housing option including sheltered accommodation and specialized housing schemes for people with physical or learning disabilities. It offers

support to enable someone to manage their day-to-day activities while living at home. This might be living on your own or living with other people with similar needs.

## Transition

The process by which a young person moves from child to adult services – this might be in healthcare or education services. The movement from child to adult services is normally planned with the young person and their family to help ensure a smooth process. Depending on the young person, planning may start a few years before the transition will occur.

# References

American Psychiatric Association. (2013). DSM-5 diagnostic classification. *Diagnostic and statistical manual of mental disorders*.

Autistica. (2019). Epilepsy – autism. Retrieved 29 June 2022, from https://www.autistica.org.uk/what-is-autism/signs-and-symptoms/epilepsy-and-autism

Babb, C., Brede, J., Jones, C. R., Elliott, M., Zanker, C., Tchanturia, K., Serpell, L., Mandy, W., & Fox, J. R. (2021). 'It's not that they don't want to access the support... it's the impact of the autism': the experience of eating disorder services from the perspective of autistic women, parents and healthcare professionals. *Autism*, 25(5), 1409–1421. https://doi.org/10.1177/1362361321991257

Bargiela, S., & Standing, S. (2019). *Camouflage: the hidden lives of autistic women*. London: Jessica Kingsley Publishers.

Baron-Cohen, S., Leslie, A. M., & Frith, U. (1985). Does the autistic child have a 'theory of mind'?. *Cognition*, 21(1), 37–46. https://doi.org/10.1016/0010-0277(85)90022-8

Baron-Cohen, S. (1997). *Mindblindness: an essay on autism and theory of mind*. Cambridge, MA: MIT Press.

Baron-Cohen, S. (2002). The extreme male brain theory of autism. *Trends in Cognitive Sciences*, 6(6), 248–254. https://doi.org/10.1016/S1364-6613(02)01904-6

Boulter, C., Freeston, M., South, M., & Rodgers, J. (2014). Intolerance of uncertainty as a framework for understanding anxiety in children and adolescents with autism spectrum disorders. *Journal of Autism and Developmental Disorders*, 44(6), 1391–1402. https://doi.org/10.1007/s10803-013-2001-x

Corbett, B. A., Vandekar, S., Muscatello, R. A., & Tanguturi, Y. (2020). Pubertal timing during early adolescence: advanced pubertal onset in females with autism spectrum disorder. *Autism*, 13(12), 2202–2215. https://doi.org/10.1002/aur.2406

Czech, H. (2018). Hans Asperger, national socialism, and 'race hygiene' in Nazi-era Vienna. *Molecular Autism*, 9(1), 1–43. https://doi.org/10.1186/s13229-018-0208-6

Doherty, M., Neilson, S., O'Sullivan, J., Carravallah, L., Johnson, M., Cullen, W., & Shaw, S. C. (2022). Barriers to healthcare and self-reported adverse outcomes for autistic adults: a cross-sectional study. *BMJ Open*, 12(2), e056904. doi:10.1136/bmjopen-2021-056904

Dudas, R. B., Lovejoy, C., Cassidy, S., Allison, C., Smith, P., & Baron-Cohen, S. (2017). The overlap between autistic spectrum conditions and borderline personality disorder. *PLoS One, 12*(9), e0184447. https://doi.org/10.1371/journal.pone.0184447

Eaves, L. C., & Ho, H. H. (2008). Young adult outcome of autism spectrum disorders. *Journal of Autism and Developmental Disorders, 38*(4), 739–747. https://doi.org/10.1007/s10803-007-0441-x

Eloise, M. (2022). *Obsessive, intrusive, magical thinking.* London: Icon Books.

Heasman, B., Livesey, A., Walker, A., Pellicano, E., & Remington, A. (2020). DARE report on adjustments. Centre for Research in Autism and Education, Institute of Education, UCL, London, UK. Retrieved 29 June 2022, from https://dareuk.org/dare-adjustments-toolkit

Hull, L., Petrides, K. V., Allison, C., Smith, P., Baron-Cohen, S., Lai, M. C., & Mandy, W. (2017). 'Putting on my best normal': social camouflaging in adults with autism spectrum conditions. *Journal of Autism and Developmental Disorders, 47*(8), 2519–2534. https://doi.org/10.1007/s10803-017-3166-5

Kanner, L. (1943). Autistic disturbances of affective contact. *Nervous Child, 2*(3), 217–250.

Kenny, L., Hattersley, C., Molins, B., Buckley, C., Povey, C., & Pellicano, E. (2016). Which terms should be used to describe autism? Perspectives from the UK autism community. *Autism, 20*(4), 442–462. https://doi.org/10.1177/1362361315588200

Lisette, C. (2022). *Eating disorder recovery journal.* London: Jessica Kingsley Publishers.

Loomes, R., Hull, L., & Mandy, W. P. L. (2017). What is the male-to-female ratio in autism spectrum disorder? A systematic review and meta-analysis. *Journal of the American Academy of Child & Adolescent Psychiatry, 56*(6), 466–474. https://doi.org/10.1016/j.jaac.2017.03.013

Milton, D. E. (2012). On the ontological status of autism: the 'double empathy problem'. *Disability & Society, 27*(6), 883–887. https://doi.org/10.1080/09687599.2012.710008

Mind. (2020). Personality disorders: Why is it controversial? Retrieved 29 June 2022, from https://www.mind.org.uk/information-support/types-of-mental-health-problems/personality-disorders/why-is-it-controversial

National Institute for Health and Care Excellence. (2009). Autism spectrum disorder in adults: diagnosis and management [CG142]. Retrieved 13 October 2022, from https://www.nice.org.uk/guidance/cg142/chapter/Recommendations#interventions-for-coexisting-mental-disorders

Neff, M. (2021). Borderline personality disorder or autism — insights of a neurodivergent clinician. Retrieved 29 June 2022, from https://neurodivergentinsights.com/misdiagnosis-monday/boderline-personality-disorder-or-autism

Opar, A. (2021). Puberty and autism: an unexplored transition. Spectrum. Retrieved 29 June 2022, from https://www.spectrumnews.org/features/deep-dive/puberty-and-autism-an-unexplored-transition

Pearson, A., Rees, J., & Forster, S. (2022). 'This was just how this friendship worked': experiences of interpersonal victimization among autistic adults. *Autism in Adulthood, 4*(2), 141–150. https://doi.org/10.1089/aut.2021.0035

Schott, W., Tao, S., & Shea, L. (2022). Co-occurring conditions and racial-ethnic disparities: Medicaid enrolled adults on the autism spectrum. *Autism Research, 15*(1), 70–85. https://doi.org/10.1002/aur.2644

Sparkes, I., Riley, E., Cook, B., & Machuel, P. (2022). Outcomes for disabled people in the UK: 2021. Office for National Statistics. Retrieved 29 June 2022, from https://www.ons.gov.uk/peoplepopulationandcommunity/healthandsocialcare/disability/articles/outcomesfordisabledpeoplein theuk/2021

Stark, E., Ali, D., Ayre, A., Schneider, N., Parveen, S., Marais, K., Holmes, N. & Pender, R. (2021). *Psychological therapy for autistic adults.* Authentistic Research Collective. Retrieved 10 October 2022, from https://www.authentistic.uk

Taylor, L. E., Swerdfeger, A. L., & Eslick, G. D. (2014). Vaccines are not associated with autism: an evidence-based meta-analysis of case-control and cohort studies. *Vaccine, 32*(29), 3623–3629. https://doi.org/10.1016/j.vaccine.2014.04.085

Vegni, N., D'Ardia, C., & Torregiani, G. (2021). Empathy, mentalization, and theory of mind in borderline personality disorder: possible overlap with autism spectrum disorders. *Frontiers in Psychology, 12.* https://doi.org/10.3389/fpsyg.2021.626353

Wakefield, A. J., Murch, S. H., Anthony, A., Linnell, J., Casson, D. M., Malik, M., ... & Walker-Smith, J. A. (1998). RETRACTED: Ileal-lymphoid-nodular hyperplasia, non-specific colitis, and pervasive developmental disorder in children. https://doi.org/10.1016/S0140-6736(97)11096-0

World Health Organization. (2018). *International classification of diseases for mortality and morbidity statistics* (11th Revision).

Xie, L., Gelfand, A., Delclos, G. L., Atem, F. D., Kohl, H. W., & Messiah, S. E. (2020). Estimated prevalence of asthma in US children with developmental disabilities. *JAMA Network Open, 3*(6), e207728–e207728. https://doi.org/10.1001/jamanetworkopen.2020.7728

Yuhas, D. (2019, 27 February). Untangling the ties between autism and obsessive-compulsive disorder. Spectrum. Retrieved 11 October 2022, from https://www.spectrumnews.org/features/deep-dive/untangling-ties-autism-obsessive-compulsive-disorder

Zeldovich, L. (2017). New global diagnostic manual mirrors U.S. autism criteria. Retrieved 29 June 2022, from https://www.spectrumnews.org/news/new-global-diagnostic-manual-mirrors-u-s-autism-criteria

# Index

vaccines 65–6
Vandekar, S. 148
Vegni, N. 141

Wakefield, Andrew 65
Walker, A. 101, 224
World Health Organization
(WHO) 117

Xie, L. 148

Yuhas, D. 136

Zeldovich, L. 28